T0179685

"Life can be challenging at any age, and spiritual practice can be beneficial at any age. However, as Lewis Richmond makes crystal clear, these benefits may be especially important and valuable with aging."
—Roger Walsh, M.D., Ph.D., University of California Medical School, author of *Essential Spirituality: The 7 Central Practices to Awaken Heart and Mind*

"Thoughtful, truthful, loving, Lewis Richmond helps us bring attention to the mystery of aging with great kindness and wisdom."
—Jack Kornfield, author of *A Path with Heart*

© PENNI GLADSTONE

Lewis Richmond is a Zen Buddhist priest and meditation teacher who has published three previous books: the national bestseller *Work as a Spiritual Practice*, *Healing Lazarus*, and *A Whole Life's Work*. He leads Vimala Sangha, a Zen meditation group, and teaches at workshops and retreats throughout the San Francisco Bay area, where he lives.

CONNECT ONLINE

www.lewisrichmond.com

AGING
as a SPIRITUAL
PRACTICE

A Contemplative Guide to
Growing Older and Wiser

LEWIS RICHMOND

AVERY

an imprint of Penguin Random House

New York

AVERY
375 Hudson Street
New York, New York 10014

Previously published in hardcover by Gotham Books
First trade paperback edition, January 2013
Copyright © 2012 by Lewis Richmond

Penguin supports copyright. Copyright fuels creativity, encourages diverse voices, promotes free speech, and creates a vibrant culture. Thank you for buying an authorized edition of this book and for complying with copyright laws by not reproducing, scanning, or distributing any part of it in any form without permission. You are supporting writers and allowing Penguin to continue to publish books for every reader.

Most Avery books are available at special quantity discounts for bulk purchase for sales promotions, premiums, fund-raising, and educational needs. Special books or book excerpts also can be created to fit specific needs. For details, write SpecialMarkets@penguinrandomhouse.com.

The Library of Congress has catalogued the hardcover edition as follows:

Richmond, L. (Lewis), date.
   Aging as a spiritual practice : a contemplative guide to growing older and wiser / Lewis Richmond.
      p.   cm.
   ISBN 978-1-592-40690-6
  1. Aging—Religious aspects—Buddhism.   2. Spiritual life—Buddhism.   I. Title.
   BQ5435.R53   2012   2011032723
   294.3'444—dc23

ISBN 978-1-592-40747-7 (paperback)

Printed in the United States of America
ScoutAutomatedPrintCode

Book design by Susan Hood

While the author has made every effort to provide accurate telephone numbers, Internet addresses, and other contact information at the time of publication, neither the publisher nor the author assumes any responsibility for errors, or for changes that occur after publication. Further, the publisher does not have any control over and does not assume any responsibility for author or third-party websites or their content.

To my wife, Amy, who first had the idea

CONTENTS

FOREWORD

Getting older, especially the limitations of being older, has always provided sure-laugh material for stand-up comedians. These days there is a proliferating array of greeting cards marketed as "Birthday," "Senior," and "Humorous." The only one I've seen that seems genuinely funny proclaims, "Getting old is not for sissies!" It's funny because it makes it sound like aging is optional and that people who do not think of themselves as heroic should reject it as a possibility. Apart from the ambiguous wording, though, the message is fundamentally valid. Aging gracefully and contentedly is a challenge.

My friend Beatrice moved into an assisted living facility when she was ninety-five. She wrote to me, saying, "Although I can still draw, my legs are too unstable and I need to be here. I wish you would come to teach a mindfulness class here for me and other friends who live here. We are all having trouble getting used to our new situation." The story of my going to teach is not relevant here except to say that the phrase that stays with me until now is "trouble getting used to our new situation."

The Buddha taught that life was challenging for everyone because of the constantly changing nature of our experience. We get used to managing, and circumstances change. At the same time that Beatrice moved into the assisted living facility, my youngest grandchild, after two years of preschool, announced that she was worried about starting kindergarten. "I won't know where to put my lunch box," she said, "or where to hang my jacket." I thought about how, from one end of life to the other, we are always getting used to our new situation.

The crux of the Buddha's teachings is that peace of mind is possible in whatever circumstances one finds oneself. During most of our lives, if we are lucky, health and vigor and the prospect of years to come all support the mind in accommodating challenges. We can endure challenges, make skillful changes in our lifestyle, relationships, or work, and look forward to less stressful times. We can accommodate without the painful imperative "This needs to be different now!" because the mind imagines it has time.

For me, accommodating the process of growing older is different from any challenges I have had in the past because I am very conscious, even though my health is still good, of running out of time. I am grateful for whatever equanimity my spiritual practice has given me, but many of my friends are sick and some have recently died. I'd like more strength and courage than I already have to be able to be with ailing friends wholeheartedly. I want to continue to cultivate enough delight in sunsets and tulips and symphonies and good movies to keep me a cheerful companion for my family and friends. I've changed one of the phrases of my blessing practice from "May I be healthy" to "May I feel strong" so that I can say it until the last day of my life.

This book is a wonderful guidebook for gracious aging. The contemplative reflections in it are profoundly moving. I hope that you not only read this book but also take its tools as part of your spiritual practice. I have a hope for myself these days that comes from a story I heard just a few years ago about a Zen teacher, a person I had known about but had never met, who had just died. She is said to have said, as her last words, "Thank you very much. I have no complaints."

Gratitude, with no complaints, is the attitude that I would like to have, not only at the end of my life, but from now until then.

May it be so for all of us!

Sylvia Boorstein

Growing
Older and
Wiser

Growing Older and Wiser

This book is a user's guide to aging well. It is not a book about diet or exercise, crossword puzzles or memory tips. Those books have already been written and offer much that is valuable and useful. This book is different. It is about aging from a spiritual perspective.

I am a Buddhist priest and meditation teacher, and spiritual practice has been the focus of my life and work for many decades. If you too are a Buddhist, then many of the contemplative reflections and spiritual lessons I write about will be familiar to you, though applying them as we do here—to benefit the aging process—will be new. And if you are Christian, Jewish, Muslim, Hindu, or some other religion, or profess no religious affiliation at all, I believe that these reflections will speak to you too, and be of use to you.

I am in my mid-sixties, so I am not a passive bystander. This journey of aging is *my* journey too. Many of the fears and worries—as well as the joys and rewards—of aging are mine also. I have had to grapple with the illness and death of parents, the sudden demise of friends younger than I, my own serious illnesses, loss of youthful vigor and sense of open-ended possibility—experiences that may be familiar to you. We are all walking this path together. It is the road that those of us fortunate enough to have lived this long must take.

The seeds of *Aging as a Spiritual Practice* were planted when I started looking for ways to connect my Buddhist spiritual life with my own experience of aging. Finding this kind of connection is something I have done before. Twelve years ago, when I was working as a corporate executive, I looked around at my work environment, observed the difficulties my coworkers had in coping with uncertainty and stress, and wondered if Buddhist meditation could help people—myself included—transform their workplace experiences.

From that seminal question came my first book, *Work as a Spiritual Practice: A Practical Guide to Inner Growth and Satisfaction on the Job*, which was published in 1999. There I offered a variety of Buddhist meditations to address common workplace difficulties: stress, pace, emotional conflict, power, worry, and stagnation. This book is arranged differently, but it too applies a variety of spiritual practices to the phenomenon of aging, and in so doing, it offers readers a way to age well.

In the process of writing this book, I started a blog. The interesting thing about a blog is that you have to write something, and write frequently. That imperative was helpful in getting me started. My first post was entitled "Everything Changes, Everything Ages," and looking back I still think that was the right place to start. That is, after all, where Buddhism starts too, as I learned from one of my Buddhist teachers, Shunryu Suzuki.

Once, after a lecture, someone asked Suzuki (we all called him "Roshi," which means "old teacher"), "Roshi, you've been talking about all this Buddhist stuff, but frankly I can't understand anything you are saying. Can you say one thing about Buddhism that I can actually understand?"

Suzuki waited for the nervous laughter to die down and then quietly said, "Everything changes."

It's not hard to understand this teaching as an intellectual fact; we learn it naturally by living it. But emotionally this teaching means that everything we love and care about—including our family, friends, and even our precious self—will change, transform, and eventually pass away. That is the first truth of Buddhist teaching, and the first truth of aging, too.

At first blush this thought might seem depressing, but the process of transformation—aging and its accomplishments—can be very positive, with new possibilities, fresh beginnings, a wealth of appreciation, and a depth of gratitude that profoundly affects how our lives proceed. These positive, often exciting, aspects of aging are what I want to share with you in these pages. I have talked with many people who are not necessarily in denial about their aging but still don't like to think about growing old. They probably do think about it—a lot—but don't know how to approach the subject with dignity and grace.

Beyond a certain age, we don't need to be convinced that we are aging and that aging has its difficulties. We all know that. But how can we do it in the best possible way, toward the very best end? This book offers an inner road map for aging, one that draws on my many years as a spiritual leader—a map that reimagines aging not as a time of decline, but as a time of fulfillment that can, in spite of occasional indignities, be something to enjoy.

When in one of my early blog posts I first used the words "enjoy" and "aging" in the same sentence, I found myself transported to a time early in my spiritual training when I was still in my twenties. I had come to a small Buddhist temple on a busy San Francisco street to hear a lecture by Shunryu Suzuki. At the time, Suzuki was in his sixties, and most of the people in the room were in their twenties and thirties.

During the question-and-answer period, someone asked, "Why do we meditate?"

Suzuki answered with a laugh, "So you can enjoy your old age."

We laughed with him. We thought he was joking. Now I realize that he was being honest. He had been ill the whole previous winter and was still coughing and wheezing months later. Physically he hadn't been feeling well, and yet his whole demeanor radiated contentment. He was clearly enjoying his old age.

I now think that Suzuki was actually letting us in on a great secret, one that the young cannot truly understand: It is possible to find enjoyment in the gift of each moment and each breath, even in the midst of difficulty.

Suzuki died not long after that. It was only then, as details of his life came out, that we discovered how full of tragedy that life had been. And yet he did not show it or let it defeat him. He met what life handed him with kindness and a ready smile. His example has been a lifelong inspiration for me, and a touchstone for the writing of this book. Many of the contemplative practices described here are ones he taught me. Even the teachings I have drawn from Christianity and Judaism come, I believe, from the same universal wisdom source that Suzuki embodied.

So I wrote about enjoying your old age in my blog, and kept writing. After receiving many appreciative and informative reader comments, I came to understand that people experience their aging in a variety of ways. Some blog readers had a good handle on their own aging and were looking for ways to navigate the aging process with more skill. Others were skeptical. One woman in her nineties remarked, "Young man, I'm not old. Aging is a myth. I don't see the point of what you are doing." Others were much younger. I had one correspondent who was twenty-seven and wrote, "I've suddenly realized that I'm growing old."

In order to expand my own horizons, I started doing some one-day aging workshops. I began at Buddhist centers, where I knew the participants would be familiar with the kind of meditation practices I taught. I came away from those early workshops with an important lesson: No matter how familiar participants were with meditation, the idea of connecting these practices to the experience of aging was new and exciting to them. At the end of my first workshop, I asked the people attending how many would like to do it again, and every hand went up.

Bit by bit, blog post by blog post, and workshop by workshop, the elements of this book slowly took shape. As you can see from looking at the table of contents, each chapter explores one facet of the aging experience. The chapters don't have to be read consecutively. If you are feeling down about growing old, start with Chapter 4, "I Like Growing Old." If you agree with the ninety-year-old skeptic who didn't believe in aging, Chapter 5, "I Don't Like Growing Old," may set you straight. The needs and interests of a forty-year-old reader are different from those of one who is eighty. Aging does progress in stages, as Chapter 2 illustrates, and locating your stage may help you use the book to your best advantage.

I have also included two chapters that review what scientific researchers, doctors, and psychologists have to say about aging. With seventy million baby boomers in their fifties and sixties, aging research is a "booming" field. Not surprisingly, physical exercise and diet are key to healthy aging; the research proves that beyond any doubt. But serving others, maintaining healthy relationships, being in nature, and having an active spiritual life—topics central to this book—are equally important. Inner and outer aging are close partners. Until we can find the inner enjoyment of which Suzuki spoke, exercise and diet alone will not suffice to make us content.

Each chapter concludes with contemplative reflections designed to cultivate some strength or talent or wisdom toward an aspect of aging. Some of these reflections use the body and breath to see through our mental constructs about aging and ease worry and regret. Some help in developing gratitude, refining our sense of appreciation, and teaching the pleasure of serving others. The reflection on "just being" is designed to put us in touch with our own divine nature: the place from which all life has come and to which all life will go. The last chapters help construct a personal "day away"—a time to sit, walk, appreciate, and renew.

"Everything changes," yes, but that truth has two sides. It is true that everything we love is destined to change, age, and pass away. But it is equally true that every moment brings with it new possibilities. We shouldn't allow our fixed ideas about aging to take those opportunities away. One of my Buddhist teachers liked to say, "Every breath, new chances." So if we say that everything changes, we should also add that everything is workable—maybe especially our old age.

Once, one of my workshop attendees raised his hand and half-jokingly said, "I'm fifty-eight and I know where I'm headed—downhill. It's all downhill from here."

I thought for a moment and replied, "Well, I'm not sure

I agree, but even if you're right, the real question is: Are you going to just slide, or are you going to steer?"

I hope this book will help you steer. I have tried to put a few stars in the sky to help you navigate. Aging is beyond our control, but *how* we age is up to us. I invite you to join me on this journey to discover how to enjoy your own aging to the fullest.

CHAPTER 1

Lightning Strikes

Youth and Old Age

Once, when I was about twelve, my father came into my room holding a book. He was in his forties at the time.

"I want to show you something," he said.

The book was an autobiography of the poet Robert Graves. On the front cover was a photograph of Graves as a young man: black-haired, handsome, and full of vitality and hope. My father turned the book over to show a photograph of the present-day Graves: hair white, face wrinkled, eyes shrouded in sorrow.

"Look at this," my father said, turning the book over and over, showing me the startling transformation of youth to old age and back again. "You can't understand this," he said. He dropped the book on my bed and just as suddenly as he had come into my room, he turned and left.

I had not said anything. I sensed my father's awkwardness and the poignancy of his effort, but he was right. I didn't really understand, any more than I could understand Suzuki Roshi when he spoke of enjoying his old age. Now, at sixty-four, I do understand and thank my father for his long-ago effort. The old understand the young better than the other way around. My father wanted to reach out across the gulf separating age from youth and tap me with the magic wand of this hard-won knowledge, but he couldn't. He could only show me the two photographs and wish the best for me as I set off on the journey to adulthood.

When Suzuki said "Everything changes," he could just as easily have said "Everything ages." That is what my father was trying to show me.

Intellectually we know this. We know that everything ages; we see it all around us. For much of our life it is like the house we live in or the air we breathe—a familiar fact that we barely notice. But as we grow older, that fact is harder to shrug off. Aging is not just change, but irreversible change—for better or for worse. We did not get that sought-after promotion, and now it will never come. Or we did get the promotion, and life has never been the same! We are poor. Or we were once poor, but now we are not. We have a bad knee, and even surgery will not make it new. Or maybe the surgery worked and we can say goodbye to the pain we'd lived with for so long. We always wanted children, but now we are too old to have them. Or we adopted a child, to our never-ending joy. One way or another, our life consists of "the things that happened to happen."

Irreversible change is different because there is no going back. Its triumphs sustain us; its losses mark us. The real question, the one this book can help you answer is: What do we do about it? In much of today's world, people are living longer than they ever have. The life expectancy at the turn of the century was forty-five; now it is eighty. Living into one's eighties, nineties, and even past one hundred is a real possibility today, one that makes your fifties and sixties a time not for winding down but for gearing up—though for what, we may not be sure. In many ways society has not yet caught up with these new facts of life, and neither have we. We need to look afresh at this prospect of a longer life and ask ourselves, What's the best use of this extra gift of time?

The answer, I propose, is that aging is an ideal time for the cultivation of the inner life: a time for spiritual practice. Why it should be so is captured in that image of the old Robert Graves that I still vividly remember. Graves' white hair and lined face seemed to tell my father a story of loss, one that he was already experiencing in the disappointments of his own middle age. But I saw something else, something that made me want to open the book and read. The face of the old Robert Graves seemed to me to be the face of a wise person, one who knew something important. I wanted to know what that was and how he had gained it. As I turned the pages and followed Graves' life story from youth to full adulthood and finally to old age, I caught an inkling of what it takes to live a rich and complete human life from start to finish. And now that I myself am closer to the end of my life than to the beginning of it, I realize that my reading of Graves' story so long ago was the beginning of my study for this book.

This book is about the connection between aging and spiritual practice. It offers many spiritual exercises, suggestions, and ideas to help you age well, but it also advances the premise that the experience of aging is itself a doorway to spiritual practice, one that transcends any particular religion or faith.

Lightning Strikes

When my father barged into my room with the Graves book in his hand, I believe he wanted to say that the dreams he had when he was young were slipping away, and where was he going? What was he doing?

My father, a self-taught man who read Greek philosophy in the evenings and thought deeply about things, had touched upon a universal truth. I have heard some version of it from many people when I talk to them about their experience of aging and I have given it a name: Lightning Strikes.

Lightning Strikes is the moment we truly wake up to our aging and can see the full significance of it in our whole life, from its unremembered beginning to its unknown end. Until that moment, regardless of our age, we spend much of the time not thinking too much about where our life is headed or what it all means. But once lightning strikes, it's different. We have reached a tipping point. We have stopped seeing things as we wished they were and, for a moment at least, can see them as they actually are.

Lightning can strike in what seems to be a disturbing or negative way, as it did for my father, or in a positive way, as it did for Katherine, age fifty-seven and chief of staff for a local politician.

As I sat in her living room one summer afternoon, appreciating the shimmering leaves of an aspen tree outside the open window, Katherine sat a bit formally on the couch, quietly answering my questions. But when I got to the question, "Is there anything you particularly like or enjoy about aging?" her face lit up, and she said, "My granddaughter!"

She was already reaching for an album on the coffee table. We spent the next few minutes looking through her album of new family photographs. It was only when she offered to get her laptop to show me more photos on Facebook that I demurred.

As the interview progressed, I asked Katherine if she could say how the birth of her grandchild had affected her view on aging.

She grew thoughtful. "This sounds odd," she said finally, "but it's made me feel as though my life has really amounted to something. Isn't that strange?" She laughed. "I didn't feel that way when I had my own children, and I've accomplished a lot in my life."

My father and Katherine represent the two faces of aging: the wrinkled face of the aged Robert Graves and the joyful smile of a new grandmother. Regret and celebration are equally important facets of aging. Throughout this book, these two aspects will appear in various guises and voices.

That was the case with Alan and Christina, a married

couple who stumbled into the thicket of aging one morning when the telephone rang.

Alan and Christina

I first met them at a fund-raiser for a Buddhist group they belonged to. They were an outgoing, friendly couple who both looked to be in their fifties. Alan was a tall, athletically built man with salt-and-pepper hair. After a few minutes of conversation I learned that he was a high school history teacher and track coach. Christina, a slender woman with a pale complexion, was a local artist who was about to open a solo show.

Then they asked what I did, and I explained that I was working on a book about aging. "Any thoughts?" I asked.

"No," Alan replied, laughing a bit uneasily. "I'm still in denial."

Christina added, "We don't like to talk about it."

We soon found ourselves talking about something else; that was the extent of our conversation about aging that evening. Yet over the next few days, I found my thoughts returning to the interchange. Here were two accomplished, intelligent people who were uncomfortable talking about a topic that may have been important to them both. And when Christina had said, "We don't like to talk about it," I was intrigued. I wondered what she meant.

So I got in touch and asked if we could continue the conversation. The following week, I found myself sitting in their living room, drinking a glass of wine, surrounded by athletic trophies and Christina's bright acrylics.

"So," Christina said as she set down a tray of snacks, "what's going to be the title of your book?"

"*Aging as a Spiritual Practice*," I said.

"That makes an interesting connection," Christina said.

"We have the spiritual practice part down," Alan said. "We both meditate every morning before breakfast." He chuckled. "Unless I sleep in. Christina is more consistent than I am."

"It helps us stay young," she explained.

"At least that's the plan," Alan said.

"Not that we're old," Christina said. "Alan still runs marathons. After two children I still weigh almost what I did in college. We were kind of planning to be young forever—until Alan got the phone call the other day," Christina said, "and we found out his college roommate had just dropped dead of a heart attack. While he was out running."

"Bill was a track star in college," Alan said. "He set the school record in the two hundred meter. Of all people for that to happen to!"

"Alan hasn't been able to do his morning run since he heard the news," Christina said.

"Don't exaggerate," Alan said quickly. "I can do it. But it creeps me out. The next morning, I tried to do my meditation as usual, but I kept thinking about Bill and his kids, and how strong he was physically, and all the good times we had together."

The three of us sat in silence for a while; then Christina said, "I feel a little different than Alan. You know I'm about to open a new show?"

"Yes," I said. "I've seen the posters."

"It's my first solo show," she said. "And I'm already talking to people in New York about showing there. Artists have to grow. My painting is better now than ten years ago. I'm still developing, and I feel myself still coming into my own. I don't care about growing old. As long as I can paint, I'm happy. It's different for Alan. He feels everything in his body. If he misses running for a day, he's grumpy."

"No, I'm not," Alan said.

"So that's where I'm headed," Christina said. "But Alan is on his own track."

"That's right!" Alan said. "I'm a track coach. What matters to me is a winning team."

"Sounds like the two of you might be in different places around aging," I said.

"I guess," Alan said. "Is that a problem?"

"I don't know," I said. "But you've both been discussing it, and you've certainly been thinking about it. I talk to a lot of people who aren't paying attention yet. Regardless of how they feel about growing old, people need to pay attention. Paying attention is one of the main things I teach."

Paying Attention

The word "spiritual" can mean many things. For many people it means their religious faith. For others it's a more generalized feeling of unity or oneness. Some people tell me that their spiritual practice is walking on the beach or sitting quietly on the couch in the morning before breakfast.

Recent polls report that 15 percent of Americans—some 45 million people—consider themselves unaffiliated with any specific religion, but do value and seek to incorporate spirituality into their lives. That tells me that spiritual experience is a common human value, and when I teach it I try to find a definition of spiritual practice broad enough to include everyone.

Paying attention to aging is important because aging itself is important. It matters. Aging, like all spiritual practice, has to do with life's fundamentals. When I teach meditation to beginners, I sometimes start by asking people to speak a word or short phrase that expresses what really matters to them: in other words, their core spiritual values. As we go around the room, the succession of words people say begins to form a connected thread—something like a poem or prayer.

FAMILY

KINDNESS

BEING A GOOD PERSON

KNOWING HOW TO LIVE MY LIFE

HELPING OTHER PEOPLE

WISDOM

DEALING WITH SUFFERING

LEARNING HOW TO BE HAPPY

LEAVING THE WORLD A BETTER PLACE THAN I FOUND IT

I have heard much the same words from people in many audiences. Why should that be surprising? These words represent universal spiritual values. Paying attention to these things that matter is the nub of spiritual practice, as the following story about Ikkyu, an eccentric fourteenth-century Japanese Zen teacher, demonstrates:

Once, a wealthy patron came to him and asked him to write a scroll of calligraphy expressing a deep spiritual truth. Ikkyu took out paper, brush, and ink and after a few moments wrote the single character for "attention."

Then he put down his brush.

Typically a Zen poem includes nature imagery, such as plum blossoms or pine boughs, and a few words of wisdom. What Ikkyu had written was not what the patron was expecting. At first the patron leaned forward, seeming to pay close attention to what Ikkyu was writing. But after waiting politely for a few moments, the patron leaned back and said, "Perhaps the master is not yet finished with his poem."

Ikkyu took up the brush and again wrote the single character for "attention" right below the first one.

Now visibly annoyed, the patron explained that he was hoping for a poem to share with the guests that often visited his home. "Many of my friends have been generous supporters of your temple," the patron added pointedly.

Ikkyu, also with a bit of annoyance, grabbed the brush and quickly wrote the same character three more times: attention, attention, attention!

Had the patron been more alert, he might have realized that Ikkyu was not just writing the character for "attention" over and over in place of a poem; he was also teaching about it. Ikkyu was saying to the self-satisfied patron, "Pay attention to your state of mind right now! Why are you here? Are you greedy? Are you arrogant? Are you ambitious? Is all you want from me something to impress your rich friends?"

Mere paying attention is not always a spiritual practice. Paying attention rises to the level of a spiritual practice only when it is about core spiritual values. Ikkyu understood the patron's true motives, and he chose to turn the moment into a spiritual lesson.

Aging usually forces us to pay attention to what is really going on. My father had to face his own disappointments. Alan had to face his own mortality. Even Katherine, when asked to think about her own aging, came face to face with her own accomplishments—and felt good.

Lightning Strikes: Contemplative Reflections

HOW DID YOU FEEL?

I know when lightning struck for me. It was when I sat in my doctor's office and he told me I had cancer. I was thirty-six years old, and until that moment I had never given much thought to growing old. I was in the prime of my life; everything was going my way. I walked out of my doctor's office utterly changed. In the time it took me to drive from the doctor's office to my house, I felt as though I had aged twenty years.

When did Lightning Strike for you? Can you think of a specific event that shifted the way you thought about aging, as it did for my father, for Katherine, or for Alan?

If you can, focus in on that memory. Jot down your thoughts as you do. Study that moment in all its detail; tune in to the feelings or emotions you had at the time.

Was the feeling positive or negative? Name the feeling; give it a word.

If the feeling was positive, did it change or shift your feeling about growing old? If it did, how would you describe that change?

Ask yourself the same questions if the feeling was negative.

When I did this exercise myself, I recalled my feeling as negative. I felt confusion and anxiety as I drove home from the doctor's office, but it was not about having cancer; it was about what I was going to tell Amy, my wife.

But when I told her, she took it in stride. She was as solid as a rock, and that gave me the strength to say to her, "Well, I'm not going to die." At that moment, I was visualizing myself living to grow old, having a long life.

How did you feel when lightning struck? And how did that feeling change your attitude toward aging?

HOW IS IT GOING NOW?

I checked in with Alan a couple of months after our interview to see how he was doing.

"How's it going now?" I asked him. "Are you running again?"

"Oh, yeah," he said with a laugh. "My fears only lasted for a few days. But every day when I run now I think of Bill. He's my friend in a whole new way. He helps me remember how good it is to be alive and to have a healthy body that can still run, and that none of us ever knows what's going to happen. I never used to think about stuff like that."

How is it going now for you? How is the moment when lightning first struck affecting your life today? Has the memory faded, or is the recollection still fresh? Have there been more such moments, each one building on the last? Write a single sentence describing how it's going now. Read it back to yourself. Has your present self fully absorbed the lessons of the past?

What spiritual lesson did you learn from the moment lightning struck?

What I would write is, That was the day I grew up.

After twenty-five years, that spiritual lesson is still alive for me. Our whole spiritual life is like that, I think. It flows like an underground river throughout our life and surfaces to help us remember what is really important and who we really are—if only we pay attention.

CHAPTER 2

Stages of Aging

"I'm twenty-seven and I've suddenly realized that I'm growing old," Howie's e-mail said. When I thought back to the time I was twenty-seven—my son had just been born and I was still in training as a Zen priest—I had never given a thought to growing old, so I had some trouble imagining what Howie meant. But I thanked him for his insight. Everyone experiences aging differently.

"I'm seventy-three and I've never felt younger," wrote Jerry in response to one of my blog posts. I could only imagine the conversation Howie and Jerry might have had if I had put the two of them together!

Some people get to sixty before they can say, "I've suddenly realized that I'm growing old." And others can live their whole life and not be able to say, "I've never felt younger." How each of us ages is individual. And yet there are recognizable stages and emotions on the journey of aging.

In the first stage, Lightning Strikes, the dominant emotion is surprise. We are taken aback to realize, "I'm really growing old," and then surprised again at how long it took us to see it.

The next stage, Coming to Terms, takes hold when we compare ourselves with how we once were—favorably or unfavorably. We look back at the "old me" and see how it measures up against today's "new me." If we like being the age we are now, that comparison brings happiness; if we don't, it leads to regret.

The stage of Adaptation comes when we no longer compare ourselves to the past and can rest in the age we are now.

And the final stage, Appreciation, comes when adaptation matures into full acceptance.

As Howie and Jerry show, any stage can arise at any age, and stages do not necessarily appear in a fixed order. Sometimes we have to traverse these emotional zones more than once.

Coming to Terms

People come to terms with their aging in a variety of ways, but one common way is when parents become ill or die. Until then, whatever our actual age, we think of ourselves as young in comparison to our parents. After all, we were once children in their homes, and somewhere in our hearts we remain their children.

But once parents become ill and need our help, suddenly we assume the role of the grown-up, and they become a little like our children—a role reversal that is unsettling all around. The drama may begin suddenly, but what follows is often a long, drawn-out march that may take months or years. That process of adjustment, whether long or short, is another example of Coming to Terms.

Anna, a successful choreographer and dance producer, experienced this when her father, and then her mother, were both diagnosed with Alzheimer's disease. Until then Anna hadn't given much thought to aging. She had a dancer's physique and the youthful vigor to go with it. Her idea of a relaxing vacation was going river rafting or climbing a mountain. She was proud to tell people her age—forty-seven—and loved hearing the invariable response, "You're kidding! You look ten years younger."

But once the twin diagnoses came from the small clinic in her faraway hometown, Anna's life changed dramatically.

"I can't tell you how exhausting it was," Anna told me as we sat in a corner of her dance studio sipping tea. "First there were the trips home, at least once a month, and sometimes more often than that. Then there were the arguments, especially with my dad. He thought they were both just fine and could take care of themselves. It didn't matter that their doctor said otherwise."

"It must have been hard to keep the studio going," I said, indicating the large dance floor.

"Oh, I managed. My dance friends filled in. The worst

thing was the fights with my brother and sister. Their idea of solving the problem was to sell the house, take away the car keys, and get Mom and Dad in a nursing home as soon as possible. And they lived right there! They actually could have taken care of them if they'd wanted to."

Anna's Coming to Terms was fraught with difficulty. "If only things could go back the way they were," Anna sighed. "I know that's impossible, but in the middle of the night that's how I feel."

She yearned for the way things were before, for her "old me," but eventually a time comes when the "old me" is finally ready to go, and the "new me" is ready to settle in. For Anna that happened the day she was talking alone with her parents' doctor.

"How long do they have to live?" she blurted.

"They're both physically strong," the doctor answered. "They could live for many years."

That's when Anna realized that her old life was gone; what she needed now was to build a new one.

Adaptation

The next stage, Adaptation, is a time when our emotional ups and downs begin to level out. We have come to terms with what we have lost. We look forward to what we still have. We know we are getting old and we have accepted it. The "new me" is here to stay, and our new job is to learn to live with it, adjust to it, and enjoy it.

For Toni Bernhardt, author of *How to Be Sick,* acceptance

dawned in a moment of tenderness and laughter with her husband.

Toni, formerly a law school dean, writes of an important moment seven years into her illness, a chronic fatigue that would not end:

> My husband [Tony] came into our bedroom and joined me on the bed that has become my home. I greeted him with, "I wish I weren't sick." Tony replied, "I wish you weren't sick." There was a slight pause, then we both started laughing. "OK, that got said." It was a break-through moment for the two of us. We'd had this exchange dozens of times since the summer of 2001, but it took seven long years for the exchanges to bring us to laughter instead of to sorrow, and, often, to tears.

As long as we keep comparing ourselves to a younger, better self (who may have been better only in hindsight), we shortchange the possibilities for becoming an older, wiser one. The wisdom of Adaptation begins in the willingness to let go of who we used to be and embrace who we are now.

In a spiritual sense, this flexibility means accepting and adapting to change. When change brings good things, we like it. When it brings bad things, we fight it. The Buddha was one of the first religious teachers to teach the truth of continuous change and its implications for a human life. Even though we are not the person we were at fifteen, twenty, thirty, or forty, some part of us clings to the notion that "I am, and have always been, me." Our inner sense of self yearns for constancy.

Central to the Buddha's message of liberation is that this constancy is an illusion. We are always changing, as is everything and everyone around us. When we are young we don't pay too much attention to this, but as we age we have less choice. Change and the steady progression of years begin to dog our footsteps, and we hear that tread behind us with every anniversary and birthday, with every letter or e-mail about a good friend who has become ill, or when a parent has passed on.

The challenge of the stage of Adaptation is how well we can adjust and remain flexible as the signs of wear and tear in our world grow more noticeable. One of the clear results of current aging research is that—physically, mentally, and emotionally—those who remain flexible and roll with the punches age the best, stay the healthiest, and live the longest.

Adaptation and flexibility are our best strategies for keeping abreast of our aging, and the keys to creating freshness and new opportunities as we age. We need to remember that change works both ways. It is not just wear and tear; it is also new beginnings.

Appreciation

The oldest person I ever interviewed was Sarah, a dignified woman of 105 who had been an occasional attendee in my meditation group. When Sarah was young she had been a schoolteacher. In her fifties she retired from teaching and took up botany. She had a talent for finding plants that others had overlooked. She became locally famous for discovering rare natives; one of them was named for her. In her seventies Sarah tried retirement but found it boring.

On her ninetieth birthday, widowed but still living in her own home, she took up weaving. Within a few years she had attained the rank of master weaver, and on the day I visited her she sat on her sunporch surrounded by wall hangings woven in her distinctive multilayered style.

As I sat down to begin the interview, I realized that I felt intimidated by her age. I had never spoken to someone so old, and I suddenly felt stupid. She was nearly twice my age.

"What's it like to be 105?" I began.

For a moment her mouth tightened in irritation. But then she relented.

"Young man," she said (how long it had been since anyone had called me that!), "look around. Look at all these." She waved her hand at the weavings that surrounded us.

"When I look at these, I'm happy," she said. "Really! I'm happy. I lived my life and I did what I wanted. You want to know what it's like to be me? To be 105 years old—as if that mattered? I made these. That's me. I did what I wanted to do."

I was embarrassed at my first question. I tried again. "What do you think is the deepest lesson you have learned in your life?"

She gave me a quick, piercing glance, and then looked down and said quietly, "This is my life; I have no other."

Not everyone comes to the end of their life like Sarah, in full possession of her faculties and doing work that gives her joy. Some people end their life disappointed. But regardless of circumstance, everyone can say, as Sarah did, "This is my life. I have no other."

When the Stages Happen All at Once

Occasionally we experience all the stages within a short period of time. I've already mentioned the moment lightning struck for me. The full story is a yearlong journey that took me through all four of aging's stages, from the shock of Lightning Strikes to deep Appreciation.

After many years of training as a Zen priest, at thirty-six I was a busy business executive and my blood pressure had been going up.

Most other doctors would have dismissed my blood pressure as job stress and given me pills, but my doctor had a hunch. He sent me for some tests, including an ultrasound, which showed that something about my left kidney didn't look right. There were more tests, then a CAT scan, and finally my doctor's pronouncement. "There's a large tumor behind your kidney. We think it's some kind of lymphoma. We have to do more tests to find out exactly what kind." My doctor cleared his throat; he was only a few years older than me, and this was hard for him too. "Lymphoma usually has a pretty good prognosis," he said in a reassuring tone. "If you have to have cancer, this is one of the better ones."

One of the better ones! What a thought! "I'm thinking about my family," I stammered. "That's all I'm thinking."

"I would be too, if I were you. But let's not jump to conclusions," my doctor said. "Let's take things one step at a time." But for me, time had suddenly accelerated to light speed and there was no "one step at a time." It was all happening at once.

I drove home clutching the steering wheel for dear life. After I told my wife, we sat at the kitchen table in the near dark, not saying much. I kept repeating, "I don't know what's going to happen."

That's how lightning struck for me—all in a rush at an age when I least expected it. That first evening, and in the days after, my life pretty much came to a stop. I couldn't think, I couldn't plan, and any efforts toward normalcy, like making breakfast or going to work, seemed ridiculous. One part of my mind kept returning to its ordinary rhythms—I would be making my morning tea and forget about my new dilemma—while another part of my mind was still running in circles, saying, "I'm going to die!" There had been a moment early on when I was sure I wouldn't die, but this part of my mind had apparently forgotten that. I was in a state of intermittent panic.

But panic can last only so long. Even though some part of me was unhinged, physically I was feeling fine—no different than a few weeks before. As the days became weeks, the routines of being a cancer patient took hold, and the panic slowly devolved into tedium. I spent hours each day in one waiting room or another, listening for my name to be called.

Slowly I came to terms with the fact that I was really ill. If

I had had any doubt, the chemotherapy treatments—one every three weeks—made me ill. I would come home after each one and lie in bed, waiting for the nausea and weakness to come. I thought about the recent past when none of this was happening and I had a seemingly normal life. I compared that person to the one I now was: the "new me." After a couple of rounds of chemotherapy I wanted nothing more than to forget about the "new me" and go back to being the "old me."

That thought is at the heart of Coming to Terms—comparing how we feel now with how it used to be.

Everyone around me was coming to terms in their own way. Amy adjusted the fastest. She has an extraordinary ability to cope with a crisis. She always seemed to know just what to do. So did my dog, Ryan. Every morning, when my wife and son, Ivan, got up to have breakfast, he got up too, while I stayed in bed. And after Amy and Ivan had left for work and school, Ryan came back into the bedroom and got up on the bed to be with me. He knew I needed to be comforted. He stayed there as long as it took for me to finally drag myself out of bed.

My son, who was nine, had been told only that I was ill and would get better before too long. He didn't question that, but he could see how weak I was and he was a smart boy. Before my diagnosis, one of our favorite games was "blanket bear." I'd put a blanket over my head and growl like a bear, and we wrestled. Now I was too weak to play.

One afternoon while I was lying in bed feeling miserable, he came into the bedroom and said, "Dad, when you get better will you still be able to play blanket bear with me?"

I assured him I would.

That's how Ivan dealt with my cancer.

As the weeks of treatment stretched into months, I became depressed. Some of that was a chemical effect of the drugs and some was a feeling that the long ordeal would never end, or if it did it would not end well. One hot summer evening, I was resting in the basement, where it was cool, and fell into a meditative state. I began an exercise in inner inquiry and "sent" a question into my body. From my Zen training I knew that the body has its own wisdom and often knows better than the mind what is going on.

The message I found myself sending was, "I hate this!"

It was a shock to admit that this was how I felt, but I did. I hated feeling so sick, hated not knowing what was going to happen, and hated admitting that was how I felt.

I kept sending my message: "I hate this, I hate this!" For a long time, no answer came. But quite suddenly, when I had almost fallen asleep, a response appeared: "I love you!"

Who said that? Who loved me?

I can't say it was me. I was busy saying "I hate this." That voice was connected to me, but it was higher or deeper. I started to cry and felt tremendous relief. The world had shifted under my feet. One moment I was watching my life slipping away and the next I felt it returning to me. I had hit bottom and was on my way back.

Emotionally, I had finally let go of the "old me," the one who didn't have cancer. Until that moment I hadn't really accepted the cancer. Part of me hated it and still wanted to go back to a time before. But some power had a message for the "old me"—and that message was, "I love you. It's all right." As a Buddhist, I would call that power "Buddha nature." Some people might call it divine presence or God. Whatever it's called, that power helped me put the "old me" to rest and open up to the "new me."

Several months later, after those long months of treatment were finally over, I sat in my doctor's office and heard him say that the cancer was gone and was unlikely to return.

"You did great," my doctor said. "You're one of the most upbeat patients I've ever had." He pulled out a Polaroid photo of me, taken during the last month of my treatment, showing me bald and grinning from ear to ear. I can't recall exactly when he took that photo or why I was grinning, but there it was.

He pinned that photo on the bulletin board of his examining room. For years afterward, whenever I went back for checkups, I saw that photo of myself: the upbeat cancer patient.

After that final doctor visit, my wife and I went back out to the car. She drove; I was too emotional. I thought back to the moment when a voice from somewhere inside me had said, "I love you." I had come to a deep acceptance of my life in a way that I probably never could have without the intervention of sudden illness.

I was grateful for everything.

Lightning Strikes, Coming to Terms, Adaptation, and Appreciation—they all happened to me in the course of a single year. After twenty-five years, my memory of that period of my life has faded. But my appreciation of it never has. I have never since taken my life for granted.

Contemplative Reflections

EMOTIONS AND AGING

Much of how we experience aging is through our emotions. When things are going well, we feel good and we like the age we are. But things can change all of a sudden and completely overturn that earlier good feeling, and vice versa.

As one example, I was in a meeting with Marcia, a fellow meditation teacher who had just received her Medicare card. She was upset. "I didn't realize it was going to hit me this way," she said. "But it threw me for a loop. I feel so old!"

At that moment Marcia was experiencing various emotions about her aging: anxiety, upset, and disappointment. Objectively, the day she received her Medicare card was just another day, but emotionally, it was a shock.

Marcia's experience is a lesson in what an emotional ride aging can be, and how those emotions can distort our experience of aging.

This Reflection is an inquiry into your own emotions around aging. What one word best describes your primary emotion about how old you are? Is it "surprise," "regret," "relief," "contentment," "gratitude," "despair," or something else? Take a moment to tune in to your emotions and give it a description or a word.

If you are feeling surprise, what has surprised you? Was it a birthday—yours or someone else's? The death or illness of someone you know? Think back to a time before that event. How did you feel then? What is different now?

If your feelings about your aging are regret, what do you regret? Regret is often a stand-in for other, more primal emotions, such as fear, anger, or anxiety. Is that true for you? Can you dig down to that deeper emotion and see if you can identify what caused it or what it is about? Each of us has some version of Marcia's Medicare card, some event, perhaps half-forgotten, that connects our aging with some powerful emotion.

If your primary emotion is positive—if you are feeling contentment or gratitude—reflect on the process that got you there. With Anna, whose parents had Alzheimer's, gratitude or contentment came at the end of a longer story, and so it is for each of us. That story is worth remembering because it is not over. Things change. New challenges will come; new stages will appear. If you are feeling contentment today, know that you may lose it, but also know that you can find it again.

In sum: Pay attention to your experience of aging through the lens of your emotions. What you feel can help you determine where you are in the stages of aging and also help you understand, as Marcia did, that emotions are not the whole story.

AGING BREATH BY BREATH

I saw Marcia again a few days later and asked her how she was feeling. She said, "Much better. I spent the weekend leading a meditation retreat, and by the end I realized how foolish I'd been. That card is just a piece of paper. It doesn't reflect anything real about how old I am. Actually I'm just getting older one breath at a time."

Marcia's final comment, "I'm just getting older one breath at a time," points to another way to experience aging, one that is outside the realm of emotion. I call it Aging Breath by Breath.

To begin, take a posture that is comfortable for you. If you are an experienced meditator who can sit cross-legged on the floor, do that. If you prefer a chair, that's fine too.

Find a quiet place to sit, one free of noise and other distractions. Now gradually tune in to your breath as though to a quiet radio station. Breathe in, breathe out, pause; breathe in, breathe out; pause.

Do this for a few minutes, and then stop and reflect. What are the qualities of the breath? Isn't your breath quiet, with a steady pulse and a reliable rhythm? In those ways is it not like a clock? In that sense, isn't it keeping time?

Now return to your breath: breathe in, breathe out, pause; breathe in, breathe out, pause.

Tune in to your breath. It is your own, actual, precious life, and in a way, your body's own natural clock. When you observe your breath, you are not just passing through time; time is also passing through you.

Stop again and reflect. How does it feel when you breathe in? Isn't there pleasure in taking a deep inhalation? Isn't that what the phrase "a breath of fresh air" means? How does it feel when you breathe out? Isn't there something deeply relaxing about it?

This is how aging feels to us when we age one breath at a time. Remember the previous exercise, when you looked at aging through the lens of emotion, and notice the difference.

Emotions are not like the breath. They are neither rhythmical nor steady. They are often neither pleasurable nor relaxing. Even if they are, emotions change, and time changes with them. When our emotions speed up, time speeds up too. When we are feeling down or unhappy, time slows to a crawl.

When it comes to aging, our emotions are not a reliable timekeeper, but breathing is. As Marcia discovered, the breath is our deepest timekeeper and is the true arbiter of how we actually age.

Now let your focus and reflection on the breath come to an end and simply sit quietly. Our thoughts and feelings about aging may rise and fall, come and go, but the way we *actually* age is simply one breath at a time.

CHAPTER 3

Elderhood

"Acceptance" describes how we feel as we mature into aging. But there is another way to talk about aging's culmination, one that focuses less on how we feel and more on what we do. I call this role "elderhood." In traditional societies, male and female elders had certain roles to play and jobs to do that compensated for the losses that come with aging. They were the ones who told the legends and stories, who knew where the medicine plants grew and what their uses were. They were guides for younger adults, and caregivers and mentors for the community's children. They also commanded respect by virtue of their having lived a whole life and knowing the full meaning of it. Even if an old man could no longer walk, or if old woman could no longer see, they could fulfill their role as elders and be honored for it. There is even a theory among evolutionary biologists called the "grandmother hypothesis," which holds that "evolution favored older women who used their knowledge and experience to benefit their relatives' children."[1]

Anyone who has visited a skilled nursing facility and seen its hallways filled with the infirm, the disabled, and the confused must wonder if this is the best we can do for our elders and if there is nothing tangible left for them to do for us. Yet it would be too simple to say that in today's media-saturated, youth-oriented society the role of elder has entirely vanished. These days, many of the elders' traditional roles have been professionalized. A person who is troubled goes to a therapist. Instead of gathering medicinal plants to cure our illness, we visit the local pharmacy. Young children are tended to in day care; the old stories are stored on Wikipedia. Today's elder generations are sometimes lucky enough to have appreciative grandchildren to mentor and occasionally care for, but even then, it is most often a very part-time job.

But in the same way that a toddler takes her first step or a young mother gives birth to her first child, elders know how to be elders when the time is ripe. As Dr. William H. Thomas says in his book *What Are Old People For*, "We do not have to think about breathing in order to breathe, and we age whether or not we wish to do so. Aging is within us, not imposed on us."[2] The basic skills of elderhood are innate. That being said, those skills can also be honed, particularly by studying with another elder. The following stories illustrate both possibilities.

Dignity

When my father, Emil, burst into my room holding the book of Robert Graves, his distress stemmed partly from the fact that there had been no older role model in his life when he was young, and no one to go to now for his middle-aged anxieties. His own father left when he was three. Young Emil grew up poor and without male guidance. That loss haunted him and made it harder for him to be an elder to me. Once, during an aging workshop, I spoke of elderhood, and afterward an Indian American man approached me and introduced himself. He was a professor of engineering at a nearby university but had grown up in a small town in northern India. "You are right about the elders," he told me. "I saw that for myself when I was young."

His parents had come from a once prosperous village in the rural foothills and wove cloth to send to market in the city. But now, that work had mostly gone to low-cost factories in China. The village had become poor and there were few jobs for the men.

"Once, when we were visiting, my father took me to sit with the men in council. I watched as the younger men implored the elders of the village to help them know what to do. The elders didn't necessarily have all the answers, but I could see how much the younger men respected them, and how much dignity the elders expressed when they spoke. Something was happening in that room that felt powerful to me. Everyone was in difficulty, but the old men gave something like medicine to the younger men. I have never forgotten that."

Integrity

In his groundbreaking 1950s book *Childhood and Society,* Dr. Erik Erikson proposed a theory—now widely accepted as fact—that the human psyche develops in discrete stages, beginning with an infant's "basic trust" and concluding with an old person's "integration." When I was in college I studied with Erikson and heard him describe integration as "the time when we have come to the point of being able to understand our place in the world and the life we have lived in it."

The class reading for integration was Shakespeare's *King Lear.* I had some difficulty with the assignment, finding it hard to see Dr. Erikson's "integration" in the character of Lear. So when Dr. Erikson came to our study session one afternoon, I asked him about it. "Lear doesn't seem to me to be a typical old man," I said. "In fact he seems kind of crazy."

As I remember Dr. Erikson's answer, he said, "Oh, he's pretty typical, I think. You need to look past the high drama. In the end he's just an ordinary man trying to come to terms with being old."

I ran into Dr. Erikson again thirty years later. He was still the same self-effacing, avuncular presence that I remembered from college. With his mane of white hair and exuberant moustache, he felt every inch an elder. Now in his eighties, to me he was not just a world-renowned author and teacher, but also an ordinary man who himself had come to terms with being old.

Watering the Roses

Mr. Pauzer came to live with us when I was about seven years old. We lived on an acre of land at the edge of the suburbs, and there was a small apartment out back that my parents rented for extra income. Mr. Pauzer was thin and frail and spoke in a near whisper. I knew little about him, but from my parents' conversations I got the sense that he was a widower and had been wounded in the war.

Even as young as I was, I sensed sadness in Mr. Pauzer. I think now that he was slowly dying of emphysema. No one ever came to visit him and he rarely went out. He must have been quite lonely, and I imagine it cheered him up to have a little boy tagging after him as he wandered around the grounds, pruning, planting, and watering—"puttering" as my mother would say.

My mother had a rose garden on one part of the property, and one summer I was given the responsibility of watering the roses. There were trenches dug around each rose bush, and channels connecting the trenches, but when I turned the hose on I could never get the water to flow smoothly from one bush to another. The water always seemed to spill out into the driveway.

One afternoon I looked up, hose in hand, and Mr. Pauzer was standing next to me. "Water flows downhill," he said in his raspy whisper. "Watch the water. Watch the way it goes."

I watched as the water spilled out into the driveway. "You see," Mr. Pauzer said, "the water knows where it wants to go. You've got to dig the trenches deeper."

He picked up a hoe that he had brought with him and showed me how to dig. Over the next few days he coached me as I dug out the trenches—sometimes by hoe, more often by hand. The day came when I turned the hose on and saw the water flow just the way Mr. Pauzer had said it would until every bush was fed by its own pool of water.

"You see?" Mr. Pauzer said. "The water knows."

Later that week I came home from school and saw Mr. Pauzer beckoning me from a distance. When I approached there was a mischievous look in his eye.

"Here," he said, dropping a piece of chocolate into my hand. "Don't tell your mother."

And then he made a sound that first seemed like coughing. When I looked up I realized that he was laughing, something I had never seen him do before.

Not long after that he was taken away in an ambulance and my parents told me that he had died. But for a short time, Mr. Pauzer demonstrated his elderhood in showing me how to water the roses.

Don't Step on That Plant!

Harry Roberts was a part-Irish, part-Yurok Indian who had spent part of his youth on a reservation in Northern

California. During that time he trained with his Yurok uncle in how to be a medicine man. When I lived at Green Gulch Zen Temple in the 1970s, Harry—by now in his seventies—served as a farm adviser, horticulturalist, and down-to-earth spiritual adviser.

One day a group of us was walking with Harry to inspect a water reservoir. Harry brought up the rear. We were all chatting among ourselves when suddenly from behind he spoke up sharply, "Stop! Don't step on that."

We all froze. Usually Harry spoke quietly, in a barely audible voice. It was a surprise to hear him talk so forcefully.

He strode past us and pointed at the path beneath our feet. "That's yerba buena. That's a medicine plant. You never step on that."

That's when I learned that Harry always watched where he put his feet.

Another time, I watched as Harry was showing my friend Richard how to weld with an oxyacetylene torch. Richard had done a little welding before and thought he knew how to do it, but Harry was teaching him a different way, a more careful way. He gave a few spare instructions and then watched in silence as Richard fired up the torch and began to work.

I didn't know anything about welding and was curious to see how Richard would do. I watched as he went about applying the flame to the thick metal plate. All of a sudden his stool shifted under him and he threw out a hand to balance himself. As he did, the torch turned and the flame passed over the palm of his free hand. Richard winced in pain.

I glanced over at Harry, sure he would say something. But Harry's face was impassive. He didn't say or do anything. Richard didn't say anything either. He knew Harry. He carefully turned off the torch, set it down, and went off to find the first aid kit.

Harry got up and left too. I remained, alone, to think about what I had seen.

In Native American culture, a teacher does not usually explain things but lets students find out for themselves. Harry had told us that was how it was with his own teacher. Shunryu Suzuki said the same thing about his own Zen training.

Olive Pits

Once, I was the attendant for Suzuki at Tassajara monastery. A visiting teacher had come and it was my job to serve tea to the two of them, along with fresh-cured olives the kitchen workers had harvested from a local tree. Suzuki and the guest each ate their olives and drank their tea, and after serving them I did the same.

While Suzuki was talking to his guest, without turning around to look he reached back, picked up one of the olive pits on my plate, popped it in his mouth, and began sucking on it. I was dumbfounded. What was going on? I glanced down and realized that on each of my olive pits there were a few bits of olive meat. I hadn't eaten them completely.

After he was through sucking on the pit, Suzuki replaced it on my plate, all the while talking to his guest and pointedly ignoring me.

I was so embarrassed that I wanted to sink into the floor and disappear. But there was no time for that. Instead I poured Suzuki and his guest another cup of tea and spent the next forty years thinking about what had happened that day.

Suzuki often spoke of his own teacher. "He never explained anything," Suzuki said. "He just scolded us when we did it wrong."

Neither Harry nor Suzuki was an ordinary elder; each was master of his respective teaching traditions. These stories tell how they taught and how the wisdom their age had granted them was revealed. I have long considered what they did and how they acted, and I have concluded that a younger person, no matter how talented, could not have done what they did. Their actions stemmed not from just knowing something, but from having lived it fully. Their responses were at once spontaneous and long practiced. I think they both embodied Dr. Erikson's description of an elder as someone who has "come to the point of being able to understand his place in the world and the life he has lived in it." Always watching where you put your feet, or eating someone else's olive in a way that makes it into a lifelong teaching are not just particular skills, but a way of being that takes a long time to grow into.

Contemplative Reflections

DISCOVERING YOUR OWN ELDERHOOD

The old men in the village in India and my childhood friend Mr. Pauzer had no special training in how to be elders; they just knew how to do it when the need arose. In a sense we could say the same about the fictional King Lear; throughout the play he rages until at last he comes to the true humility of his years—an insight that has little to do with his being king. In contrast, Harry Roberts as a youth trained with spiritual mentors, and Shunryu Suzuki did the same.

There are many possible ways to express elderhood. What are yours? This contemplative reflection encourages you to explore this question.

First, reflect on whether there was a Mr. Pauzer in your childhood—an elder who stepped forward to help you when you needed it. You might need to jog your memory; until I sat down to write this chapter I had forgotten how Mr. Pauzer taught me to water the roses. An elder is different from a parent. Often parents don't know about the elders in their child's life. My parents never knew how Mr. Pauzer helped me; that is a piece of what made him special and memorable for me.

Elders from childhood are early models for our own aging selves. Make a list of your childhood elders. Write down their names and next to each name write a word or two to describe their gift to you. Next to Mr. Pauzer's name

I would write the word "confidence." Next to Harry's name I would write the word "alertness." Next to Suzuki I would write the word "thoroughness." Who are your elders and what are your words.

Next, sit quietly and contemplate the question, Am I an elder? If you are, then ask, In what ways do I function as an elder in my life?

If you are not, why not? Do you think you're too young? See if there is something you can do—and a person you can do it for—that will allow you to practice elderhood, even in the smallest way?

Finally, write these words:

BABYHOOD

CHILDHOOD

TEENHOOD

ADULTHOOD

PARENTHOOD

ELDERHOOD

And next to these words write one or two adjectives that best describe the flavor of that time in your life; if you have never been a parent, describe how you imagine parenthood might have been for you.

What do these descriptors tell you about the full expanse of your life and where you are in it?

And if you do not feel that you have lived long enough for elderhood, write instead a word that describes how you might want elderhood to be once you arrive there.

As King Lear himself said, exhausted from all his inner turmoil and reconciled at last to his youngest daughter, his tender old age, and final elderhood:

> *So we'll live, and pray and sing, and tell old tales, and*
> *   laugh*
> *At gilded butterflies . . .*
> *And take upon us the mystery of things*
> *As if we were God's spies.*

CHAPTER 4

"I Like Growing Old"

In researching and writing this book, I have learned a simple truth: Some people like growing old, and some do not. I had e-mailed an old friend, Stephanie, asking her how she felt about aging, and she replied, "Let me tell you how getting older is for me. I'm fifty-three and I love being the age I am! I'm doing a job I really like, I can wear what I want, and I don't have to worry what people think! I'm grateful for the life I have now."

That was Stephanie's short list of reasons why she liked growing old. My own list isn't long. I love being healthy; given my medical history, that is a big deal to me. My son, age thirty-seven, has a successful career and a rich social life, and that makes me happy. I am happily married to my wife of forty-two years, who has always been there for me no matter what.

I have asked any number of people what they like about aging, and I have heard many different answers:

DOING WHAT I WANT

GRATITUDE

HAVING WEEKENDS AGAIN

THE KIDS ARE OUT OF THE HOUSE

TIME TO TRAVEL

A CHANCE TO PURSUE MY DREAMS

VOLUNTEERING

GIVING BACK TO THE COMMUNITY

A SMALLER WARDROBE

TIME TO SEARCH FOR THE MEANING OF LIFE

NOT HAVING TO LOOK ATTRACTIVE ALL THE TIME

SPENDING MORE TIME WITH THE PEOPLE I CARE ABOUT

Sometimes people just exclaim, "This is the happiest time of my life!"

That's essentially what Stephanie said too. But I knew that she hadn't always been so happy. What made her so buoyant? I looked forward to a face-to-face meeting so I could hear her story.

Stephanie

We met in a coffee shop and I could see she looked different. She was wearing hoop earrings and a turquoise and silver necklace. Her hair was longer too. The last time I saw her, her hair was done up and she was wearing a pantsuit.

When I commented on how relaxed she looked, she said, "I am now."

"Now? What changed?"

She laughed. "A new job. A new life. A new way of looking at things."

And she proceeded to fill me in. She and her husband had split up two years before. And just recently she had quit a job that she had hated for years.

"What was that like?"

"For about five minutes I felt great. Then it hit me. I was making good money, I just got divorced, we're in the middle of a huge recession, and I just quit."

"That took courage."

She laughed. "Right. Then I went into the bathroom and threw up."

"What happened next?"

"I got a job in graphic design for half the money, sold my corporate clothes on eBay, and started shopping in consignment stores. Oh, and I got a dog. My ex never liked dogs."

"Lots of changes," I said.

"I was lucky; things worked out," Stephanie said.

Changes

Things change. For the usual person this is very discouraging. You cannot rely on anything. You cannot have anything. And you will see what you don't want to see. So you [have to] change the foundation of your life. "That things change" is the reason why you suffer in this world and become discouraged. [But] when you change your understanding and your way of living, then you can completely enjoy your life in each moment. The evanescence of things is the reason you enjoy your life.[3]

Shunryu Suzuki

Stephanie hadn't read Suzuki's book—she wasn't even a Buddhist—but her story is a good example of Suzuki's teaching. Stephanie's life wasn't working. Things were changing for her, and not in a good way. She was indeed finding it very discouraging. Suzuki described her situation well when he said, "You cannot rely on anything. You cannot have anything. And you will see what you don't want to see."

But Stephanie found, as she said, "a new way of looking at things." She left behind being a victim of change and became an agent of change. The changes she made in her life looked risky to an outsider. By any ordinary standard, her life was less secure than before. But by embracing change and taking charge of it, she found a way to enjoy her life.

Happiness Research

In 2010, psychologist Arthur Stone of Stonybrook University conducted a large study, polling 340,000 people on happiness, and found that people in their fifties are generally happier than those who are younger. He said, "People's overall satisfaction with their lives showed a U-shaped pattern, dipping down from the early thirties until about the age of fifty before trending upward again." Why are older people generally happier? The researchers weren't sure, but they had some ideas: Maybe older people are better at managing stress than younger ones simply because they have more practice at it. Another theory was that "older people might focus less on what they have or have not achieved, and more on how to get the most out of the rest of their lives." That all made sense to me. While you are building a career, taking care of small children, dealing with the stresses of jobs and relationships, life can indeed be difficult.

When I read about this study I called Stephanie and asked her if she knew why she felt happier now than when she was younger, and she told me that she had come to realize that wanting what she couldn't have was getting her nowhere. "All these things I wanted were driving me crazy. Now I'm not so interested in wanting what I can't have."

That's what Suzuki meant when he said you have to "change the foundation of your life." We can't escape life's essential problems, but we can, in Suzuki's words, "change our understanding" about them.

These ancient insights are being confirmed by a new research specialty called "happiness research." The Stony-brook study is one example, and there are scores of others. Taken as a whole, this research has identified three factors that tend to encourage lasting happiness: "reframing" difficult experiences (looking at things in a new way, as Stephanie did), generosity, and gratitude. Generosity and gratitude are familiar concepts; what is revealing about the research on them is the measurable increase in contentment not just in the receiver of these gifts, but in the giver as well. "Reframing" is a bit more difficult to define, but basically it means to shift your attitude about a situation from pessimistic to optimistic—in other words, the power of positive thinking. It really works! The Dalai Lama has said, "If science disproves some aspect of Buddhist teaching, Buddhism will have to change." In this case, Buddhism doesn't need to change, because it teaches these same causes of happiness: looking at things in a new way, generosity, and gratitude.

Christina

The opening for Christina's gallery show was jam packed. It took me several minutes to work my way through the crowd to the refreshments table, and even longer to spot Christina, who was in the back surrounded by a group of admirers. I started a slow tour of her bright acrylics, mostly still lifes and sunny landscapes, and noticed that several of the paintings already had red dots next to them, indicating that they had been sold. It was not until I was halfway around the room that I noticed the sign: 15 PERCENT OF PROCEEDS WILL BE DONATED TO THE FOUNDATION FOR ART IN THE SCHOOLS.

I waited for the crowd to thin out until I finally had a chance to talk briefly with Christina.

"Thanks for coming," she said. "I'm glad you could see it."

I congratulated her on her artistic success and on her

generosity in sharing her proceeds with our local nonprofit. She told me she was "paying forward," helping artists coming up, as her high school art teacher had helped her many years ago. "I'm trying to acknowledge the connection between past, present, and future. Everything is connected," she said.

Then I asked about Alan. I hadn't seen him at the show. "He'll be here," Christina said. "He had a track meet."

"How are things going?" I asked.

"I guess you could say I'm happy and he's working on it."

Christina hadn't given me her list of the reasons she was enjoying her aging, but "giving back to the community" and "doing what I want" would probably be on it. Like Stephanie, she was taking risks and moving her life forward. I wondered whether Alan and their marriage would stay abreast of it.

Everything Is Connected

Christina's comment that "everything is connected" was a message from one meditator to another; as a Buddhist I knew what she meant. She was referring to the core Buddhist teaching that we don't exist by ourselves, but depend for our existence on everything else. This is what Shunryu Suzuki meant when he once said, "Wherever you are, you are one with the clouds and one with the sun and the stars you see."

When I was young I loved hiking in the mountains, where I did feel one with the clouds. I liked being away from everything and being surrounded by quiet. I would imagine how nice it would be to live in the mountains, away from cities, smog, noise, and clutter. Then one day as I was working my way down a steep slope, I suddenly realized how foolish I was to think I was alone. I couldn't even take one step without air to breathe. My canteen was full of water from a nearby stream. My backpack was full of food I had bought at the health-food store. All my friends knew I was here and were awaiting my return. If I didn't show up, they would come looking for me.

"Everything is connected." It's a basic Buddhist teaching, and I'd studied it in books, but it wasn't until that moment in the mountains that it hit home to me and I realized that it wasn't just a concept; it was my life. Without other people, without plants and animals, without air and water, there would be no me. It was more than a feeling of being connected. I realized that the world and everything in it were all of a piece.

Without her encouraging teacher, there would be no solo show for Christina. Without a close circle of friends who supported her every step of the way, there would be no new life for Stephanie. The research shows that generosity is a cause of lasting happiness, but it doesn't say exactly why. The full explanation may be complex, but we know how we feel whenever we act generously. Generosity renews our connection with the larger world and with the reason why we are here at all. Our spirits are lifted and we are more willing to take risks.

When Stephanie's friends advised her to "hang on to that

job; hang on for dear life!" she didn't listen; she went ahead and took that risk. She sensed a different lifeline, a deeper connection. She explained to me, "I had friends; I had skills. I studied graphic design in college and I'd kept up in the field. I knew my friends in the design business would help get me started. I wasn't alone. It was still a risk, though. I still get goose bumps when I think about it."

When Suzuki spoke of "changing your understanding and your way of living," he was acknowledging the role of taking risks, in life and in spiritual practice. This too is fundamental Buddhism. Siddhartha the Buddha took a risk too when he walked out on his life of privilege. According to the traditional story, he was twenty-nine years old (middle-aged for his time and place) and living in his palace when he decided to give all that up for the robes of a spiritual wanderer—one of history's great career changes! Siddhartha's could be anyone's story. Each of us comes to moments in life when we can choose either to retreat or to take a leap. It seems harder to leap the older we get; aging tends to make us risk-averse.

Christina's path seemed different, but not really. An artist takes inner risks. Failure and obscurity are always possibilities. Many artists never have a one-person gallery show in their entire career. Stephanie and Christina were about the same age, and though they had never met, they were fellow travelers nonetheless. Each in her own way had found a path to enjoy life in every moment.

Gratitude

Emma was also an artist, twenty years older than Christina, with penetrating blue eyes and a bright spirit.

"How do you feel about aging?" I asked her.

"I feel grateful."

"For anything in particular?"

She showed me her hands, gnarled and swollen from arthritis. "I'm grateful to still be able to paint. For a long time I didn't think I would."

She also told me that two of her friends had recently died, another was in the advanced stages of cancer, and she was having to change the way she painted because of the difficulty she had holding the brush.

"When I was young I took so much for granted. I never thought about growing old. Now that I am old, I think of that saying, 'Youth is wasted on the young.' If I knew then what I know now, I would have lived my life rather differently, I think. But that's the way life is. We never know what we know until we know it, and then there's no point looking back.

"In some ways I think my painting is better than ever, because I have had to simplify and stick to essentials. I can't use my technique as much."

We were sitting in her studio, and she pointed out a recently completed work, a watercolor of a sunset over coastal mountains. "Before, I would have worked to create more texture, more detail strokes in the heather and the coyote bush. Now I can't. But it doesn't matter. Every sunset means another day of life. That's the gift of this painting for me."

Gratitude was at the top of the list of why Emma could enjoy her aging, but so was her search for meaning. When she painted a sunset, it was not just a sunset. When she picked up a brush, it was more than a brush.

Joan Chittister, a Benedictine nun, has written an excellent book about aging titled *The Gift of Years*, and I thought of Emma when I read this passage from it:

> We have every right to live in gratitude for all the stages of life that brought us here, for all the memories that give us great joy, the people who helped us get this far, the accomplishments we carved on our hearts along the way. These experiences cry out to be celebrated. They are no more past than we are. They live in us forever.

We usually define gratitude as how we appreciate things. Yet when my Buddhist teacher Suzuki spoke of gratitude, he said, "Gratitude *is* this moment." Some people thought this was because his English wasn't so good, but I don't think so. He knew what he wanted to say. Gratitude is not just appreciation; it is part and parcel of our being here. We don't need to pluck gratitude off the shelf and draw it close. It is already close.

Contemplative Reflections

THE GRATITUDE WALK

These days I walk for two reasons: for exercise and for gratitude. I am particularly taken by the dogs I meet. Dogs are so alive and alert, and they all seem so happy to be out. The very smells in the air are enough to make them grateful. How easily satisfied they are! How can I be more like them?

A gratitude walk is for noticing, and it can't be done in a gym or on a treadmill. It needs to be in nature, or at least outdoors. As I set out, I hold the thought of gratitude close and notice what catches my eye. I remember a famous Chinese monk of old who bowed to everything. He bowed to the tree; he bowed to the stone; he bowed to the rabbit running across the road. He was grateful; he appreciated each thing he saw.

I have discovered that almost anything can inspire gratitude—a tree, a leaf, a bird, a cloud, and especially a dog.

I take a notebook and pen with me while I walk. That way I can take note of what I see and consult it later. The gratitude portion of my walks is not long—ten minutes on average. Since I pet and talk to all the dogs that I meet, I don't cover much distance. But I invariably come back refreshed. One summer morning, I saw a blackberry bush bursting with fruit, and a bit later two squirrels squabbling over an acorn. I noted them, but it was not until I returned home that I was able to understand why I felt so gratified to see them. The blackberry bush reminded me that sweet things come even after a harsh winter. My long recoveries from illness taught me that; the blackberries were a poignant reminder. And the squirrels reminded me how silly it is to argue with people over small things.

I encourage you to make a gratitude walk your daily habit. If you walk regularly for exercise, as my doctor keeps telling me I must, the first five or ten minutes of it can be for gratitude. Those few minutes of thankful reflection will do as much for your mental and spiritual health as the rest of the walk will do for your body.

My friend Barbara walks for gratitude as well as for exercise, and when I told her about my love for dogs, she told me how much she loved the trees and watching them change with the seasons.

"They're just living their life," she said. "One day at a time. The seasons just happen, without anyone having to worry about it or plan it in advance. That inspires me. Now that I am retired I want to be more like that."

PEBBLES OF LIFE

I am indebted to Paul, a fellow Zen priest, for this reflection on the preciousness of human life.

I was visiting his house one day and saw a bowl full of pebbles next to a Buddha statue on a shelf. "What are these?" I asked.

"That's the rest of my life," Paul replied.

"I see," I said, not seeing at all.

He laughed. "No, really. Each pebble in there represents a week of the rest of my life."

"How many do you have in there?"

"About a thousand," he said. "That's the number of weeks until age eighty."

He went on to explain. "One day I was thinking that I was getting older, and I didn't really know how long I'm going to live. Usually I don't think about it that much. But human life is so precious. I wondered if I could be more conscious of that.

"I have this big gravel driveway. So I counted out the pebbles into the bowl. Every Monday morning after my meditation, I remove one pebble and put it back in the driveway. One week gone; who knows how many left to go."

"A mindfulness practice," I said.

"Yes. I don't always feel so good when I put that pebble back in the driveway. The pebbles only move in one direction. But a few weeks ago my wife told me that every so often when I'm not around she takes a pebble from the driveway and puts it back in the bowl."

"That's sweet," I said. "So you don't really know how many pebbles are in there, do you?"

"Nope," Paul said. "It's a mystery."

Inspired by Paul, I made up my own bowl of small pebbles from the gravel path in my garden. At first I was a little dismayed to see how few pebbles represented seventeen years. Then I reached into the bowl, dug down, and let them sift through my fingers. Suddenly it seemed like quite a few.

It all depends on how you look at them.

THE THANKSGIVING PRAYER

How many times a day do I say "thank you"? Ten times, twenty, perhaps even fifty? I was sitting alone in my armchair reading when I had this thought. I started to say thank you to myself, over and over: thank you, thank you. At first it seemed mechanical and self-conscious. But soon I found that every time I said "thank you" some picture came to mind. Thank you—and I would think of the tasty dinner I had just had. Thank you—and I noticed the book in my hand, and thought of the author who wrote it. Thank you—I glanced out the window and saw the streaks of red cirrus clouds in the setting sun. It was like taking a gratitude walk in my head, and I needed only this two-word phrase to call it up. I was like the Chinese monk who bowed to everything.

This was my thanksgiving prayer.

Try it now.

THE FEELING OF GRATITUDE IN THE BODY

When I was repeating the words "thank you," I had a sense of pleasure and lightness. My skin felt pleasantly alive; every muscle felt relaxed. It was a wholesome feeling.

Gratitude is one of the measurable causes of happiness. Scientists using an MRI scanner have shown that a part of the brain's frontal lobe lights up when we feel it, and this feeling in my body was the proof of that. Each of these reflections on gratitude—the gratitude walk, the pebbles of life, and the thanksgiving prayer—can create that wholesome feeling.

How does your body feel when you are grateful? Next time you are grateful, tune in to your body and see. Is gratitude a cause of happiness for you? If it is, then reminding yourself of what you are grateful for can help you cultivate happiness in many situations, even when life hands you hardships, as it had for Stephanie and Emma.

This is the kind of happiness Suzuki meant when he said, "You can completely enjoy your life in each moment. The evanescence of things is the reason you enjoy your life." I have to confess that the first time I read those words I was dubious. Evanescence is the passing away of all we love. How can it be *why* we enjoy our life? Stephanie discovered that her long-standing marriage was evanescent; Emma discovered the same thing about her agile fingers. Was having those things pass away really the reason they could enjoy their life?

Yet that's what they both said. Suzuki's teaching is true. Letting go of what is already slipping away is how we actually enjoy our life.

CHAPTER 5

"I Don't Like Growing Old"

It's true: Some people like growing old, and some don't. Those that don't have their own reasons:

LESS ENERGY: PHYSICAL, SEXUAL, EMOTIONAL

PEOPLE I KNOW GETTING SICK AND DYING

I'M STUCK WITH WHAT I'VE GOT

WORRIED ABOUT MONEY

MY LIFE DIDN'T GO THE WAY I THOUGHT

PILL BOTTLES ON THE KITCHEN TABLE

THE WHOLE WORLD SEEMS TO BE GOING CRAZY

I'M GETTING FAT

Greg was an executive in a large technology company. He was high-energy, ambitious, and singlemindedly focused on his career.

When I asked him how he felt about growing old, he said, "I don't like it!"

I asked him why.

"Well for starters I chose the wrong career."

Greg explained that he had wanted to become a psychologist, but his father objected, "What kind of money is there in that? You should go to business school. Get a real job. Make some money."

"So that's what I did," Greg said. "But it's not what I wanted. Each time I got promoted, I thought, 'Now I've really made it. Maybe now I can move on.' But I never did. I should have stood up to my dad and followed my own way. But he was a tough guy to stand up to."

Greg's story is another example of "the things that happened to happen." In his case, those things had led to disappointment, but as I listened to him I wondered if anyone's life really goes according to plan. Probably not; and what is a "life plan" anyway? It is nothing more than an imagined future. Greg had once imagined a future as a psychologist, but even if he had done that, who's to say that he would have been any happier?

Greg's unhappiness seemed to stem from a comparison between the life he had imagined and the life he had, but I wondered if that was the only reason.

It didn't take long for the real reason to emerge.

"I hate seeing the best part of my life slipping away," Greg continued, "and thinking about getting old and sick, and dying angry and bitter like my dad."

Greg's father had died just two months earlier, and during

that period Greg spent many hours sitting at his father's bedside in the hospital. "I sat there listening to him go on and on about all his disappointments and realized that my life was slipping away too. His life hadn't worked out, and neither had mine."

As is so often the case, Greg was coming to terms with his own aging through the death of a parent. Now I understood. When Greg answered my question about aging by saying, "I don't like it!" the negativity of his response was driven by grief.

The Mustard Seed

There is a well-known Buddhist teaching about grief called "The Parable of the Mustard Seed." In this story a bereaved woman named Krisha comes to the Buddha with a dead baby in her arms and pleads to the Buddha to bring her baby back to life. "I've heard you are a great teacher and healer," she cried. "Please cure my boy!"

The Buddha nodded and told Krisha she was wise to come to him for help. "I can help you," he said. "There is a medicine that can assuage your grief. But there is an important ingredient in it that you need to find for me." The Buddha then asked Krisha to go into the village and take one mustard seed from any house where no one had ever lost a child, parent, spouse, or friend. "Even one mustard seed like that is enough for me to make the medicine," the Buddha said.

Krisha, excited at the prospect of the Buddha bringing her son back to life, readily agreed.

Krisha then went from house to house, still holding the

dead baby in her arms, and explained her request. At each house, people took pity on her and said, "Here, take all the mustard seed you want, but in this house too, alas, many people have died: sons, daughters, parents, nieces, nephews, cousins, everyone. There is no help for it. That is the way life is!"

Krisha heard this story at every house she visited. Growing more and more discouraged, she sat down by the side of the road and despaired. "Is there no one," she thought, "who can give me the mustard seed to take back to the Buddha? Is there no hope?"

Suddenly, as evening came on, in a flash Krisha understood. There was no mustard seed to be had as the Buddha had described. Grief is universal. The secret ingredient to the Buddha's medicine was to be found not outside, but in her own grieving heart.

Krisha rushed back to tell the Buddha of her insight, and once he had heard her tale, he nodded and smiled.

"Yes," he said. "Now you understand. Now you realize the truth of the way things really are. Now go bury your son with all ceremony and respect, and know that your grief is everyone's grief, your heart is everyone's heart. That is the true way to restore your son to the living."

This story is a good example of reframing. The Buddha refashioned the mother's grief not as an individual injustice, but as a universal tragedy. Today, a grief counselor or a support group would do much the same. The mother's grief did not vanish, but the container for her grief became larger. The Buddha, being a skillful teacher, did not just announce this insight to Krisha. He sent her forth to discover it for herself. As a psychotherapist once said to me, "It doesn't matter if the therapist knows it. What matters is that the patient knows it."

The mustard seed story also illustrates the Buddhist approach to the losses of aging. Like Greg and like Krisha, each of us carries our own individual burdens as we grow old. Taken separately, those burdens may seem unjust. "Why was I stuck with such a difficult father?" Greg was thinking. "Other people had loving fathers."

"Why did a cruel fate strike my baby," Krisha thought, "when all around me I see mothers carrying healthy babies in their arms?"

As for Greg, I was interested in what Dr. James, a psychiatrist, might have to say about his situation.

"Male, middle-aged, and lots of losses," Dr. James responded when I described Greg's situation to him. "I often see people like your friend."

"How do you help them?"

"It depends. If they show signs of clinical depression, then medication can help. More often, time and talking heals them. I try to get them to take an interest in helping someone else in need. Volunteering in a nursing home often does the trick. The truly old have a lot to teach people who are middle-aged."

The Buddha's remedy for Krisha was much the same. He encouraged her to reach out to others, going door to door and talking with her neighbors about their common grief. In that way, her suffering was healing for herself and for them.

Some Things Can't Be Fixed

Greg's own psychiatrist had prescribed antidepressants for him. Greg took them for a while, but stopped. "They helped some, but not enough," he said. "A pill can't fix this."

Greg had a point. We live in an age of medical miracles. Whether it's a faulty heart valve, a sagging jawline, or middle-aged disappointments, we tend to believe that science can fix it. While that may be true for the faulty heart valve, some things in life are not fixable. That was one lesson in the mustard seed story.

But there was a deeper lesson: Why should we see our life as broken at all? The very notion of "fixing" may itself be the problem. At the root of every discouragement is a comparison: things *should* be different, things *could* be different, and because they are not, I am disappointed, I am discouraged.

In *Zen Mind, Beginner's Mind*, Shunryu Suzuki writes about problems that can't be fixed, about suffering that we can't escape.

> Suppose your children are suffering from a hopeless disease. You do not know what to do. You cannot lie in bed. Normally the most comfortable place for you would be a warm, comfortable bed, but now because of your mental anguish you cannot rest. You may walk up and down, in and out, but that does not help. Actually, the best way to relieve your mental suffering is to sit in meditation, even in such a confused state of mind . . . There is no other

way for you to accept your problem and work on it. If you have no experience meditating with this kind of problem, you are not a Zen student. When you are sitting in the middle of your own problem, which is more real to you? Your problem or you yourself? The awareness that you are here, right now, is the ultimate fact.

Suzuki's teaching may seem harsh. In fact, when I first read it when I was young, I had no experience of that kind of suffering and was affronted when he said, "You are not a Zen student." I wondered how I could ever live up to his high standards. Yet Suzuki ends with a compassionate clue: "The awareness that you are here, right now, is the ultimate fact." At the time, I didn't really understand what he meant by an "ultimate fact," but now I do. Now I have experienced in my own life the kind of suffering he spoke of, and as a priest I have counseled people whose children were indeed dying from a hopeless disease. Most people middle-aged and beyond know this territory all too well. Suzuki was not being harsh, just realistic. He also offered a remedy: Sit in meditation, even in such a confused state of mind.

Suzuki picked an example of suffering that cannot be fixed. In doing so he was making the deeper point that running away from any of our problems—tempting though that might be—does not really help. The only thing that really helps, he says, is to find some ground to stand on, understanding that "you are here, right now."

Greg told me that when his father awoke in his hospital bed he would stare off into space and mutter that Greg had been a disappointment to him. I suggested that perhaps his father had been delirious and may not have known that Greg was even there.

"That's what the doctors said too." Greg shrugged. "But that didn't make it any easier."

I understood that. And now that his father was gone, there was no more chance for reconciliation. His psychiatrist had recommended a grief support group. Greg tried it for a while but stopped going. "It was useful, as far as it went," he said. "But it didn't help me get over my sadness. I need to find some joy in my life, and I wasn't finding it there."

Long ago when I sat in the basement thinking about my cancer, saying to myself, "I hate this, I hate this!" I was just like Greg: frustrated, angry, sad, and frightened. And when the voice from beyond myself responded by saying, "I love you," I was experiencing Suzuki's "ultimate fact." Even if you are to die from this hateful cancer, the voice said, I love you. Even if you never see another morning, the voice said, I love you. Love doesn't care about circumstance. Love cares only that you are here, right now.

Suzuki's "ultimate fact" was what helped me turn that corner. To the voice that said "I love you" it didn't matter that I had cancer. It didn't matter that I hated it or that I didn't know whether I would live or die. That voice of love stood by me unconditionally, as love always does. I'm with you, it said. However you are, or whatever happens, I'm with you.

Greg needed to hear that same voice and embrace that same ultimate fact. How would he do it?

What Can Be Done?

Greg was not a Buddhist, nor had he any other religious affiliation. He had only a passing familiarity with meditation. Suzuki's advice to sit in meditation was not really an option for Greg. Besides, as a business executive, Greg's approach to any problem, business or personal, was to find an expert to fix it. So he was dissatisfied with his current doctor and was already looking around for a new one.

Suzuki recognized Greg's dilemma when he said, "You may walk up and down, in and out, but that does not help." Possibly a new doctor would do better for Greg, but I wondered whether any professional could address Greg's fundamental problem. Suzuki could have been speaking to Greg when he said, "Which is more real to you? Your problem or you yourself?"

That teaching is not just for Buddhists. It is universal advice that points us back to ourselves, that encourages us to trust our own inner resources. It doesn't mean to ignore help from outside. Greg needed counsel, perhaps even medicine. When we are suffering, we need any help we can get. Greg had tried reaching out to others, but somehow it still wasn't the right or sufficient medicine for his difficulty.

Greg still needed to understand what it meant for him that he was "here, right now," and to experience the healing power of that realization. Whether we are Suzuki's Zen students, listening to his teaching, or we follow a different faith or none at all, this fact still holds.

I asked Greg whether there was anything I could do to help.

"Make me twenty years younger and get me a new career," he said.

"Right," I said. "But all I can offer you is what I have. I teach about aging. I give workshops on it. You might want to try one. You'll meet lots of people there like yourself."

"Well, I've tried pretty much everything else," Greg said. "What have I got to lose? Maybe it'll help."

I explained that he wouldn't be required to participate any more than felt comfortable. If he liked, he could just sit in the back and listen.

To my surprise, the next month Greg did come to a one-day workshop. He didn't say much; mostly he just listened. I caught up with him at the end of the day and asked him how things had gone.

"It was good," he said.

When I asked him if there was anything during the day that he particularly liked, at first he was noncommittal, but when I pressed him, he said, "I thought the teaching on vertical time was really good. Something clicked for me in that."

Contemplative Reflections

HORIZONTAL AND VERTICAL TIME

To age means to feel the passage of time. It is a little like driving down a long desert highway. Each day or month is a passing road sign. We remember where we were, imagine where we might be going, and have the distinct sense that the car keeps moving faster and faster. I call this kind of time "horizontal time." Horizontal time begins in childhood—or rather the childhood we remember—and continues through adolescence, young adulthood, full maturity, and beyond. The story doesn't end today; it continues around the bend toward various imagined futures.

Greg was caught up in his own horizontal time. His road signs read, YOU CHOSE THE WRONG CAREER; THE BEST PART OF YOUR LIFE IS ALREADY GONE; NEXT EXIT, SICKNESS.

There is another kind of time I call "vertical time," which means this present moment: this room, this book, this body, this breath. While horizontal time is largely mental, vertical time is more physical and is expressed in the body and breath.

Unlike horizontal time, vertical time has no before and after. It is always just here. It doesn't have room for memories or imagined futures. Memories and futures are like beads on a string; they roll into view one after another. Vertical time is more like the string itself.

THE CONTEMPLATION

To begin, sit comfortably, cross-legged on the floor or in a chair. Try to keep your back straight. Your back provides the "vertical" in vertical time. After you get settled, close your eyes and imagine your life story as a road stretched to the left and right, with your past on your left and your future on your right.

To your left, imagine the major events of your life as road signs—such as retirement, your last job, children, marriage, college graduation, and so on back to childhood. Then stretching off to the right, imagine a likely future, with corresponding road signs leading into the distance.

This is horizontal time. You can even lift your arms for a moment to feel that extension to left and right, representing the road of horizontal time.

Most of us carry this picture in our minds all the time. It helps define who we are. Notice the difference in the texture of past and future. The past is fixed; there is no undoing it. Its road signs are clear and sharp. The future is fuzzy and full of uncertainty; its road signs are blurred.

Now let your arms drop and open your eyes a little. See where you are, and feel your body. Feel the line from the top of your head to the bottom of your spine. Your body is rooted in vertical space.

Just as you pictured horizontal time as a road stretching to left and right, now picture your breath as a column moving up and down. Breathing in, feel your breath rising from the bottom of your cushion and chair. Breathing out, feel it sinking down to the same place. Up and down, rising and falling, the breath travels vertically.

This vertical movement doesn't go anywhere in space. It doesn't move from a certain past to an uncertain future. It just rests continually in the same spot. In contrast to a vehicle on the highway of horizontal time, vertical time is like a house resting on a foundation. It is solid.

Even in vertical time, regret and worry do not disappear. But they are no longer the only possibilities. When we include vertical time—the timeless conviction of the present moment—we can find relief from the signposts on horizontal time's highway.

Notice too that vertical and horizontal are not separate.

They meet in the center of the body. At every moment, we exist simultaneously in horizontal and vertical time.

GREG AND VERTICAL TIME

I checked in with Greg a couple of weeks after the workshop to hear more about his experience of vertical time and why he liked it.

"It was interesting," he said. "Horizontal time seemed really familiar, but vertical time was new. I had the feeling of discovering an old part of myself I had forgotten."

He then described the feeling of lying on his back, floating on a raft on a quiet lake. He explained that he used to do that as a child when his family spent summers at a lakeside cabin. "I remembered how nice that feeling was. I'd lose myself completely just watching the clouds."

"How do you feel about growing old now?" I asked. "Any different?"

"Well, when I remembered that feeling on the lake, I didn't feel so old. In fact, I felt young." He thought for a moment. "I guess old and young are more a state of mind than a rock-hard fact."

Over the next few weeks Greg began to feel lighter, less burdened. He had started going to jazz concerts again, a once passionate interest that he had all but given up. He also gave up looking for a new doctor and decided to stick with the one he had.

"He wants me to start dating again," Greg said. "The very thought gives me the willies, but I don't know. I might try it. It would sure beat being alone all the time."

TIME AND THE TEA LADY

Long ago, Suzuki told us that the reason we meditate is to enjoy our old age. What he meant should be clearer now. He was not talking about some way to magically erase our suffering. In horizontal time our life is what it is, and our suffering continues. Greg understood that when he said, "A pill can't fix it."

Suzuki meant that we can enjoy our age in vertical time. And contemplative work can help us understand how to enjoy each moment of vertical time, regardless of what has happened in the past or what may be about to happen in the future.

Likewise, when Suzuki described the essential teaching of Buddhism by saying, "Everything changes," he meant that everything changes in horizontal time. In vertical time, things are just as they are. We can't compare them with how they were before or how they will be after.

One of Suzuki's favorite stories to illustrate this point concerned De Shan, a Zen monk of ancient China. De Shan was a scholar of a Buddhist scripture called the Diamond Sutra. De Shan carried a bag full of commentaries on the Diamond Sutra wherever he went and was famous for having mastered them all.

One day he stopped at a roadside teahouse tended by a wizened old woman. De Shan set down his backpack full of Buddhist texts and waited while the lady prepared tea.

As the tea lady was about to set the cup of hot tea in front of De Shan, she paused and said, "Aren't you De Shan, the famous scholar of the Diamond Sutra?"

"Well, yes," De Shan said. "I am."

"You know," the tea lady said, "I'm just a poor, uneducated person, but there is a passage from the Diamond Sutra that has always puzzled me, and I wonder if you can explain it."

"I suppose," De Shan said, eyeing the cup of tea. "What is it?"

"Well," the woman continued, "it says in the Sutra that past mind can't be grasped, present mind can't be grasped, and future mind can't be grasped."

"Yes, it does say that," De Shan said. "So what is your question?"

"Well, venerable sir," the woman said with a sudden glint in her eye, "with which mind will you drink this cup of tea?"

De Shan thought for a moment and was thunderstruck to realize that although he had recited and studied this passage from the Diamond Sutra for years, he really did not understand it. He could not drink the tea in the past, for the past was already gone; he could not drink the tea in the future, because the future had not yet appeared. And the present was in continuous motion, with the past flowing into the future in every moment. The deeper teaching of the Diamond Sutra, he realized, was not something the intellect could grasp. De Shan hurriedly left without drinking his tea. Soon after, he burned all his Diamond Sutra commentaries and entered a Zen monastery for further training.

Past, present, and future mind are all aspects of horizontal time. The vehicle of horizontal time is always moving. There is no opportunity to stop for a cup of tea or anything else. In horizontal time there is no way to grasp anything, whether past, present, or future. We can no more locate ourselves in time than a bird in the sky can locate itself in space. Everything changes; everything is in motion. In vertical time, however, everything is accessible; every possibility is restful and free.

Contemplations
on Aging

CHAPTER 6

The Science of Healthy Aging

I decided to write this book because I sensed that spiritual practice and healthy aging go together. Now it seems that science agrees. Dr. Roger Walsh, professor of psychiatry at the University of California, Irvine, has recently written an article summarizing this research.[4] He began by noting that aging-related diseases such as heart disease, obesity, diabetes, and cancer are all affected by lifestyle choices. This itself is important news for anyone in the second half of life.

Dr. Walsh then listed eight lifestyle factors that have been shown to contribute to healthy aging. These include exercise, diet, time in nature, relationships, recreation, stress management, and service to others. As soon as I saw this list I realized that a spiritual approach to aging and modern research had a lot in common. And when I read the last factor—religious and spiritual involvement—I was sure of it. Ancient Taoists and Buddhists combined meditation, exercise, diet, herbs, and minerals to support long life. Clearly they were on to something! Modern research points us in the same direction.

Stress Management

Alan, the history teacher and track coach, called me a few weeks after our interview to tell me that he had joined a meditation-based stress-reduction class. "I went back to my doctor and he said my blood pressure was up. He asked me if anything had changed in my life and I just laughed."

As a meditator, Alan was already familiar with the use of meditation for stress. Using a method of mindfulness meditation developed by Dr. Jon Kabat-Zinn and explained in his book *Wherever You Go, There You Are*, many teachers of mindfulness-based stress reduction are working throughout the country in hospitals, clinics, skilled nursing facilities, and mental health centers. Alan was able to find a class at a hospital near the school where he worked.

I was interested to read a recent article[5] that defined meditation as an awareness practice that focuses the mind and trains the attention, leading to feelings of calm and well-being. It went on to say that meditation is a worldwide practice found in every major religion.

How much has changed since the days when I began meditating in my college dorm room! At that time meditation was little known or understood.

My college adviser called me into his office one day and cleared his throat. "Mr. Richmond. It has come to my attention that you are burning incense in your room and doing . . . *meditation*." He said the word with distaste.

I hastily assured him that I was up to nothing nefarious. "I'm a philosophy major," I said. "I'm specializing in Neoplatonism."

Somehow that explanation seemed to satisfy him, although I soon got rid of the incense.

Today meditation in its various forms is discussed on *Oprah*, explained in airplane safety booklets, and taught in thousands of books, magazine articles, websites, and retreat centers. Meditation has arrived. Western science has scores of medicines for blood pressure, anxiety, and stress, but Alan didn't want to take a pill and convinced his doctor to let him try meditation first. The *American Psychologist* article supported Alan's choice, noting that "several hundred studies over four decades" confirm that meditation can help with conditions such as high blood pressure and lead to "feelings of improved self-control and self-esteem." Each of the contemplative reflections in this book are a form of Buddhist-based meditation, and each offers a centuries-old path to easing worry, developing acceptance, and deepening wisdom. Modern science, which has numerous ways to objectively measure stress, confirms that meditation really works—without drugs or other outside intervention. Buddhist methods alter our mental state from the inside, making us more self-reliant in dealing with our own problems. Shunryu Suzuki liked to say that meditation was a way to make us "the boss of everything." That was his lighthearted way of saying that we can have confidence in our own inner resources.

Time in Nature

I have always loved being in nature. My first spiritual experiences were in a forest near college, and even today I maintain my connection with nature through such practices as the gratitude walk.

When I was a college student I took nature for granted. Mine may be the last generation in the industrialized world that feels that way. Now, all over the world, people increasingly spend their time in artificial environments: office buildings, underground malls, apartments, and even homes. For many, the closest they get to nature is a corner window or a houseplant. This "global experiment," in Dr. Roger Walsh's words, has costs, and he lists them: disruptions of mood and sleep, impairment of attention, and greater cognitive decline in the elderly. The multimedia world of television, Internet, and cell phones further separates us from nature.

The boomer generation grew up without computers, iPods, and cell phones. In fact, we invented them. But we have now embraced them and are surrounded by them. Facebook, originally developed for teenagers, has seen its greatest growth among people over fifty. At a time when the over-fifties need the restorative power of nature more than ever, we are spending more of our time online.

A recent *Harvard Health Letter*[6] reminds us that "Light tends to elevate people's mood, and there's usually more light available outside than in." It cites recent research in England on "green exercise" that showed health benefits from exposure to the color green in the outdoors.

It seems obvious when you think about it. We evolved in nature, and our spiritual feelings of oneness and worship come from nature. All of the world religions were founded in rural settings. Judaism, Christianity, and Islam were born in the desert, where the herding of sheep and the cultivation of grain shaped people's lives. Hinduism and Buddhism came from the tropical forests of India, where a hermit could live on fruit and nuts and needed no more shelter than a large tree. The Buddha achieved enlightenment under a tree.

How many of us today have ever met a shepherd, separated the wheat from the chaff, or picked fruit in a tropical forest? How many of us have grown up in a village where all the generations lived together and where elders taught children the skills of life? In many parts of the world, people still live this way, but even there, cell phones are common and things are changing.

Nature helps us age well because it nurtures us; that's why we call her Mother Nature. Spiritual practice was once intimately bonded with nature. Today there is an iPhone application that will set up an altar for you and ring a chime to begin and end your meditation. On *Second Life,* the virtual reality website, your "avatar" can "visit" a Buddhist temple and hear a talk on meditation from a wise beetle or a space-age robot.

Ours is a new world, and who knows where it is heading? I once made my living as a software designer, and I confess to being something of a techie. I also spent several years in a mountain monastery without telephones or electricity, absorbing the spiritual teaching of "Great Nature," as my teacher called it. Both experiences are now a part of me. The techie part maintains my Droid smartphone calendar, but for spiritual sustenance I invariably return to Great Nature.

There is a movement among environmental scientists called the "biophilia hypothesis" that says we need regular exposure to nature just to maintain normal mental health; without it, our minds don't function well. Maybe this explains why, when I ask people what they don't like about aging, so many of them reply, "The whole world seems to be changing so fast." People in their fifties and sixties today remember a time when nature and the great outdoors were right at hand. I myself spent my childhood in the outer suburbs; there was a vacant field next door to my house. I loved that vacant field and used to spend hours exploring it or lying on my back in the tall grass that would grow there in the summer until it was mowed for hay. Recently I went back to visit. The whole neighborhood is now a shopping center. That vacant field is now shared by a KFC and a Jack in the Box.

Standing there in the parking lot, I mourned for that vacant field.

Religious and Spiritual Involvement

I recently came across an article that reviewed more than seven hundred scientific studies looking at the correlation between religious involvement and physical and mental health and was stunned to discover that those who attend religious services at least once a week tend to survive *seven* years longer than those who don't.[7] This is especially true when religious involvement includes service to others. The study did not distinguish between type of religion, or whether it was meditative or contemplative. Any kind of religious or spiritual involvement was included.

During my training, I spent many years attending religious services several times a day, and for more than thirty years I have led meditation groups that meet from once to several times a week.

I never knew that my lifelong pursuit of meditation had such a practical value! I'll be sure to let the members of my religious community know about this extra benefit. What this result tells me is how essential and important a spiritual life is for basic well-being, and how much we all need it.

But why is that so? These days many people feel disconnected from the religion of their childhood. I know many people who think of Sunday morning as an ideal time to surf news sites, update their Facebook page, and catch up on their e-mails. At the same time, the latest Pew religion research polls show that millions of people are interested in spiritual matters, though they are adherents of no particular religion.

Shunryu Suzuki, in describing Zen practice, said, "In our practice, we rely on something great, and sit in that great space."[8] I find this sentence beautiful because with a slight change in vocabulary it could refer to any religious practice. Someone could say, "In our religion, we rely on God and sit with God." God is something great, or as St. Anselm defined God, "that than which nothing greater can be conceived." A Buddhist would have no quarrel with St. Anselm's language. Suzuki would have welcomed it.

As for living seven more years, that result would seem to be connected to relying on something greater than ourselves. Ninety percent of the world's population engages in religious practices, says Dr. Walsh. So nearly everyone relies on something great. In one sense, age is a time of diminishment: Growing old, we have less energy—physically, sexually, and emotionally. But relying on something great counterbalances this diminishment. As we become individually smaller, the greatness that is within us can become greater. Just as the research on the benefits of meditation did not distinguish between the many kinds and styles of meditation, the research on religious involvement did not distinguish by faith. Whatever our style, whatever our faith, all spiritual practice contributes to healthy aging, where all of us may sit in that great space.

Service to Others

Modern research affirms what all religions have known: Service to others brings gifts to oneself. As the Dalai Lama put it, "If you're going to be selfish, be wisely selfish, which means to love and serve others, since love and service to others bring rewards to oneself that otherwise would be unachievable."[9] If scientific validation of this truth is needed, there are a number of studies that provide it.[10] People who volunteer their time are happier, healthier, and may live longer.

Because I have had many illnesses, I am often asked for advice by people with chronic or intractable disease. This is never easy. What do you say to someone who is ill and will probably never recover? In the midst of my own illnesses, there was a time when I was inconsolable. None of the good advice people gave me really hit home, and I used to think, "What do they know, really?"

Now what I say to people is what I have come to know from responding to other people's pleas for help—that a positive thing about being sick is that it can be a gift to others. I urge them to reach out to someone who needs their help.

In reading the research on service and aging, I found this comment: "If giving weren't free, pharmaceutical companies could herald the discoveries of a stupendous new drug called Give Back—instead of Prozac."[11]

Fortunately for all of us, it is free, and it gives in all directions—to ourselves, to those we help, and to invisible recipients in the larger web of generosity.

Diet

Dr. Walsh's article mentions three aspects of a healthy diet: fresh fruits and vegetables, fish as a primary protein source, and reduced calories. As to the last, Dr. Robert Russell, the president of the American Society of Nutrition, recently wrote that while the public is aware of obesity's health risks, "that awareness has not translated into major behavioral change."[12] In other words, while many of us diet to keep our weight down—I certainly do—we are met with limited success. Studies comparing the various diet regimes such as Weight Watchers, Atkins, and Zone show that all of them work—for a while. The problem is staying on them.

I love to eat. All my years of Zen training haven't changed that. Dr. Russell explained that this isn't just my problem. We've all evolved, he said, to store calories that we don't need right away. Dieting means "working against the way our bodies have been programmed." Even though keeping my weight down is a challenge with each passing year, my Zen training has helped me in one area: bodily awareness. Meditation helps me "tune in" to my body and listen to what my stomach is telling me.

The stomach has two main jobs: to digest our food and to signal us when it has had enough. That signal needs a while to reach our brain, often as much as fifteen or twenty minutes. Meanwhile, that signal can easily be overridden by emotion—a fact well understood by the snack food industry. The emotional override of a piece of chocolate or a bag of potato chips is strong. If we are feeling sad, anxious, or lonely, the override is even stronger. If we think of that override as a kind of static interfering with the stomach's fullness signal, it is possible for our awareness to cut through that static.

Michael Pollen, in his bestselling eating guide, *Food Rules,* points out that many cultures have incorporated this sensitivity to the stomach's fullness into their eating customs, and even into their language. The Japanese, Pollen says, have an expression for fullness that translates as "80 percent full." The French say, "I have no more hunger." They don't say, "I am full," but simply that the feeling of hunger is gone. As with many healthy principles, there was a time when this sense of conscious eating was well-known.

Try it the next time you are eating. Make it a point to "listen" to your stomach. From time to time ask your stomach, "How are you feeling? Have you had enough?" The stomach's answer will be a sensation—often rather subtle—of fullness. Notice as you do this that there is another signal vying for attention: a voice saying, "More! More!" That voice is the emotional static. The static is usually stronger and louder than the stomach, but with practice and focus it is possible to hear the stomach's honest answer.

This is an awareness practice, and I try to do it whenever I eat. Sometimes I can hear what my stomach is really saying, sometimes not. I am continually impressed by how difficult this practice is. Sometimes I tell myself that I am on the ELF diet: Eat Less Food. Other times I give up in frustration and just eat what I want.

And when all that fails, I do what many people with iPhones and Android phones have discovered: There are smartphone applications that work as online calorie counters for the diet-conscious. I use one on my Droid called

"Calorie Counter," and there is one for the iPhone called "Tap and Track."

Millions of people in the second half of life are engaged in this same struggle, fueling a multibillion-dollar diet and weight-loss industry. Whenever I see a clip of an old movie showing a thin Fred Astaire dancing with an equally svelte Ginger Rogers, I know it didn't used to be this way. They probably didn't have to diet. Portion sizes were smaller then, they clearly exercised as part of their daily lives, and the fast-food nation wasn't born until the mid-1950s. In the meantime, we must all keep trying to eat healthy foods, to eat less food, and to listen to the stomach. Use your "gut feeling" to tell you what you need to know.

Actually, sensible eating is a good practice at any stage of life, but it is particularly true in the second half of life. As Dr. Walsh's article makes clear, all the research convincingly shows that the three biggest killers as we age—heart disease, cancer, and diabetes—are all closely correlated to weight, stress, and diet.

Flexibility

I was speaking with Dr. James, a psychiatrist whose patients were mostly over fifty. I said, "In your experience, what is the single most important factor for healthy aging?"

"Flexibility," he answered. He didn't just mean limber joints, although that helps too. He was referring to mental flexibility, the ability to adjust and adapt to physical, mental, and emotional changes as we age.

John, in his seventies, and Sybil, in her sixties, were putting their house on the market, one in which they had lived for more than thirty years. It was a multilevel, rustic home on several acres of unspoiled wilderness, and I knew how much they loved it.

When I asked them why they were selling, Sybil said, "We're both getting old. We're healthy now, but anything could happen. If suddenly one of us can't climb all these stairs anymore, we don't want to have to deal with the problem then. We want to deal with it now when we can."

John added, "Sybil and I intend to get very, very old together, and this house with all these stories isn't a house to get old in. We're healthy now, but I'm thirteen years away from being ninety, and one slipup on the stairs could change everything for our future. So while it still can be an adventure, and while we can still handle a big move like this, we're going for it."

John and Sybil are a touching example of what Dr. James means by flexibility. It's especially impressive when a married couple can come to such a conclusion together. That doesn't always happen.

In contrast, Alan's high blood pressure was a sign that his difficulty adjusting to his own aging was causing stress. Like so many people, Alan had built his career and identity around a picture of himself as young, capable, and vigorous. Hearing about the sudden death of a friend his own age challenged that picture and forced him to bump up against his own fixed ideas of himself. Going to the stress-reduction class was a wise move for Alan, a first step to help him toward the possibility of flexibility and change.

Emma is another good example of someone who discovered a new flexibility to accommodate her advancing arthritis. Artists have a knack for it; they often have an ability to see fresh possibilities where others cannot. I asked her if she had any secrets to share about her success in adjusting to her arthritis. She wasn't sure, but she did tell me about how her friends tried to comfort her by comparing her to Matisse, another artist who found a way to keep painting in spite of physical disability.

"Well, I didn't want to hear about Matisse!" Emma said. "How did that help me? I still had to find my own way. Nobody else could do it for me."

As she was speaking, she dropped the brush she was holding onto the floor. I bent to pick it up but she shooed me off.

"Let it be," she said. "I don't need it now."

Contemplative Reflections

CULTIVATING FLEXIBILITY

As we age, we become less spontaneous and impulsive than when we were young, and tend to develop well-honed routines. In part this is because by the time we are fifty or sixty our tastes have matured and we know what we like and what works for us. For example, every morning I toast large-grain couscous, mix it half and half with four-grain cereal, sprinkle it with sesame salt, and eat it with a poached egg. I've had a lifetime to try other breakfasts, and this is the one I like best. These kinds of routines help busy lives run more efficiently and flow more pleasantly.

However, there is another kind of routine that reduces our capacity to be flexible, which Dr. James said was the single most important factor for healthy aging. Routines of this kind can ossify and make us less able to adjust to aging's inevitable changes. Rigidity reduces pleasure and possibility in our life and closes doors that need to remain open for aging to blossom.

I experienced this while I was healing from encephalitis, a nearly fatal brain infection that sent me into a sudden two-week coma when I was fifty-two. The doctors never found out exactly what caused my illness, but in the days before its onset, I had a bad mosquito bite, one that made my whole arm swell up. Once I was out of rehab and recuperating at home, I developed a phobia of going outside, particularly during the mosquito season, which lasts several months in California. Even though there was no proof a mosquito had caused my encephalitis, I had read that mosquitoes *can* cause it—through West Nile virus and similar illnesses—and I developed an irrational fear that if I went outside, I risked getting the dread disease again.

It was only when I realized how much I had impoverished my life and my enjoyment of time in the garden or park that I went to work on my phobia. Phobias, like many rigid habits, are irrational; you can't will them away. But logic can help. I took out a pad and paper and created a question-and-answer exercise for myself.

I wrote:

Do I know for sure that a mosquito caused my illness? Answer: No.

What are the chances of a disease like West Nile virus causing encephalitis? (I asked my doctor about this). Answer: 1 in 50,000.

Can I wear a hat, a long-sleeved shirt, and mosquito repellant during mosquito season? Answer: Of course!

Which is stronger, my fear of the dreaded illness coming back or my desire to have a normal life with normal enjoyments? I wasn't sure about this one for a while. I had to do some real soul-searching to finally convince myself that the answer was on the side of returning to my normal enjoyments.

Medically, by this time my encephalitis had long since receded. Emotionally, I had acquired a rigid attitude that was keeping me in a fearful state. But I overcame it, finally. Taking a hike at the height of summer on a favorite trail by the seashore with Amy at my side and a backpack full of lunch goodies was the moment of my final healing.

So as this chapter's contemplative reflection, I ask you to inquire of yourself where some rigidity of your own may have set in. Have you recently had an injury, illness, or accident that has made you unable to function as you once were able? Are you upset and angry that because of a bad knee you can no longer run, that because of a bad elbow you can no longer play tennis, that because of arthritis you can no longer play the piano?

Have you suffered a trauma that has made you fearful? Are you like Linda, an old friend of mine who suffered an episode of work-related carpal tunnel syndrome through overuse of a computer mouse? Even though the condition healed, the stress of the experience made her unable to use, or even look at, a computer without feeling sick to her stomach.

Once you have identified your own fear or rigidity, begin by taking comfort in that fact. It happens to all of us. As a second step, logically take stock of your situation. Take out a pencil and paper as I did, and write down the questions you need to ask yourself, together with the answers. You may think it is unnecessary to actually write them down this way, but the act of writing carries its own power. Rigid habits and fears have their home in the dark corners of the unconscious. Writing and reading back what you have written shines the light of awareness on the dark corner.

Try it and see.

You may need to work on your problem for days or weeks, particularly if some of the questions you ask yourself do not have ready answers. Don't try too hard to come up with answers. Go easy on yourself. The unconscious sometimes needs time to be convinced that it is all right to let go, to be flexible again.

At some point, the answer is likely to come to you. It could be in a dream; it could be when you wake up suddenly in the middle of the night, while you are taking a shower, or while you are having a cup of coffee in the morning. In Linda's case, she figured out that if she put the computer, the keyboard, and the screen up on the highest shelf in her library, it didn't bother her anymore. She couldn't reach it, but she felt emotionally that it could reach her (or hurt her). She lived with it that way for a few weeks and finally took it down.

Her fear was gone. She switched it on, she typed, and she went online and watched an old Laurel and Hardy skit on YouTube.

"I never laughed so hard in my life," she told me.

Facing our own rigidities can be poignant. In "Happy Anniversary," an episode of *The Cosby Show* that I fondly remember, Dr. Heathcliff Huxtable buys his parents cruise tickets to Europe to celebrate their forty-ninth wedding anniversary.

> "We really appreciate this, son," his father said. "But we can't go."
>
> "Why not?" Dr. Huxtable asks.
>
> "Well," his father said haltingly, "For one thing, we'd miss being able to open the front door and get *The New York Times* every morning. We really like that. We'd miss the *Times*."
>
> "And I'd have to clean out the refrigerator of all that food I just bought," his mother added.
>
> "And my oatmeal!" his father added. "I wouldn't be able to have my oatmeal."

Of course there was more to it than that. Dr. Huxtable's parents were old and frail. They were afraid of taking such a long trip at their age but couldn't admit it, even to themselves. During the half-hour show, Dr. Huxtable tries various strategies to convince his parents to go. Nothing seems to work. Finally, his parents are back in their own home, sitting on the couch, thinking about the cruise. His mother muses, "That young, handsome soldier I married would have taken me to Europe."

"That's right!" his father agrees. "In an instant. So let's go. Let's not even tell Heathcliff we're going."

"We'll send him a postcard." The mother laughs.

Undoubtedly, there is something in your life that is like that cruise to Europe. Can you too find a way to broaden your thinking and overcome the limitation of habit?

When it comes to being more flexible, there is always something you can do.

CHAPTER 7

What Buddhism Teaches

Sometimes I ask Buddhist audiences, "When you think of Buddhism, what's the first thing that comes to mind?"

"Meditation," they say.

"Life is suffering."

"Enlightenment."

"Compassion."

"Loving kindness."

When I ask non-Buddhist audiences the same question, they often aren't sure. And when I ask them, "Do Buddhists believe in God?" only a few hands go up. Since Buddhism is my faith and the primary source of inspiration and practice for this book, I thought it would be a good idea now to review the basics of what Buddhism actually teaches, both for Buddhists and for non-Buddhists. Buddhism has been a dominant faith in Asian countries for centuries, but outside of ethnic communities it is still relatively new in the West, and there are a number of misunderstandings about what Buddhism actually is and what it teaches. Many people who call themselves Buddhists came to it as adults and first learned about it from the more than ten thousand books on Buddhism in English—or increasingly from websites. Some of those books and websites are about meditation, but many are not.

Buddhism Is Not Just Meditation

There are about 370 million Buddhists in the world today, and the majority do not meditate—at least not traditional silent, sitting meditation. Most Buddhists chant the name of or pray to Buddha. Buddhists also attend services, recite scriptures and prayers, and follow Buddhist ethical teachings. But even for many monks in Buddhist countries, regular meditation is unusual. This may surprise people in the West, where there is great interest in Buddhist meditation.

I once attended an interfaith wedding led by a rabbi. After the ceremony I introduced myself and said I was a Buddhist priest. "Oh, really?" he said. "Do you know Sylvia Boorstein?"

I said that she was a good friend, and he told me how grateful the local rabbinical community was to Sylvia for teaching them Buddhist meditation.

"Judaism once had its own rich tradition of meditation," the rabbi said. "It was centered in Eastern Europe and

Russia. But its teachers were all killed in World War II. Sylvia helped us rediscover our roots."

Every religion has its form of contemplative practice. Though Buddhism has many meditation practices, it is first and foremost an ethical teaching and a way of life. I have heard anecdotally that Thich Nhat Hanh, the Vietnamese Zen teacher, was once asked to summarize all of Buddhist teaching in one word. He said, "Ahimsa," which means "non-harm" or "nonviolence." This is the first ethical precept of Buddhism. The term is thousands of years old and goes back at least to the Vedic Hinduism of ancient India. Mohandas Gandhi made ahimsa the centerpiece of his doctrine of nonviolence.

When the Dalai Lama says, "My religion is kindness," he is saying much the same thing. More fundamental even than meditation for Buddhists is the sense that all life is sacred, and all life is one. That is the doctrine that underlies nonviolence. If all life is related, then we avoid harming others as much as we avoid harming ourselves. Thich Nhat Hanh calls this connection "interbeing." Shunryu Suzuki Roshi said, "When you feel the oneness of everything, you naturally don't want to harm anything."

This is the Golden Rule, spoken as a Buddhist. To practice ahimsa is to follow Buddhist values, whether you call yourself a Buddhist or not. Meditation grows out of the ahimsa spirit and is a central expression of it. The application of Buddhist meditation to aging, as we are pursuing in this book, is another application of the ahimsa spirit. Our increasingly fragile and infirm bodies and minds are sacred, and worthy of the greatest kindness and care. To respect our aging at every stage is the greatest kindness we can offer to ourselves and those we love.

Enlightenment Is Not the Main Thing

Shunryu Suzuki once said, "It is not that satori [enlightenment] is unimportant, but it's not the part of Zen that needs to be stressed."[13]

The Buddha was said to have been enlightened under the Bo tree 2,500 years ago, and ever since then, enlightenment has been a centerpiece of Buddhist teaching. It was certainly the centerpiece of my fascination with Buddhism when I first began my study in 1967.

Yet Suzuki says enlightenment is not the point that needs to be stressed. Why would he say that? Probably because it's something we want too much. That kind of desire is the opposite of what enlightenment is. Enlightenment is not something to have; it is something to live. An enlightened life means to live in mindful awareness, expressing compassion in each situation.

Someone who can truly embody the deep meaning of non-harming may be said to be living a life of enlightenment. Someone who can express kindness in each activity, as the Dalai Lama teaches, is truly practicing the Buddha's way.

The Buddha Did Not Simply Teach "Life Is Suffering"

My thirty-seven-year-old son, Ivan, sometimes tells his friends that his father is a Zen Buddhist priest. "Oh, that 'life is suffering' thing," they often reply. "I could never get into that."

Buddhism is not "that life is suffering" thing, although that is how it is often understood. Anyone who visits a Buddhist country like Japan, Burma, or Thailand will be struck with the kindness of the people and their ready smiles. They do not seem to be dwelling on "life is suffering." Ivan's friends would be closer to the mark calling Buddhism "that kindness thing."

However, the Buddha did teach the Four Noble Truths, the first of which says, "Human existence is marked by *dukkha*." *Dukkha* is frequently translated as "suffering," though "frustration" or "disappointment" might be closer to the actual meaning. This teaching does not mean that life is *only* suffering; it means that suffering is unavoidable, but that we can work to avoid unnecessary suffering. *Unnecessary* suffering is the kind caused by selfishness, fear, and greed. The Buddha taught that selfishness just makes our suffering worse, and when we are unselfish and loving, we can accept even the greatest difficulty. This is an important lesson, as it applies to aging. Some aspects of aging are difficult and cannot be avoided, but a positive mental attitude can brush away the cobwebs of much anxiety and fear.

Buddhism and God

Once, when I was on a live radio show being interviewed by a Christian talk show host, her first question to me was, "Do you Buddhists believe in God?"

I had only a few seconds to think of an answer.

"Yes," I said.

"Good!" the host said. "And how do you pray?"

I said that we prayed in silence to reach our divine nature.

"I like that!" the host said.

If I had said no to the first question, that would have narrowed the conversation considerably. But I didn't say yes just because my host was Christian. Given a choice between yes or no, I think yes is truer to the essential spirit of Buddhism. Some Buddhist teachers might not agree with me. But it all depends on what we mean by God or Buddha. Buddhists the world over pray to Amitabha or Tara—forms of Buddha who hear the prayers of anyone who calls their names. When my teacher was becoming ill, and in what became the last year of his life, he said to us, "I ask Buddha to give me ten more years." That sounded like a prayer to me.

St. Anselm saw God as beyond any thought or idea. Suzuki Roshi said, "We have to believe in something which exists before all forms and colors appear."[14] The Dalai Lama says, "If someone shows genuine love and compassion toward fellow human brothers and sisters, and toward the Earth itself, then I think we can be sure that that person truly demonstrates love for God."[15]

This principle of God as expressed by Suzuki and the Dalai Lama is what I meant when I answered the talk show host. And when it comes to aging well, I believe that such a universal spiritual expression is more important than any specific vocabulary or religion. The Dalai Lama seems to agree, saying:

> When young . . . an individual might feel completely self-sufficient, completely in control, and thus conclude that no deeper faith or understanding is necessary. But with time, things inevitably change; people get sick, grow old, die. These inevitabilities, or perhaps some unexpected tragedy that money can't fix, may clearly point out the limitation of this worldly view. In those cases, a spiritual approach . . . may be more suitable.[16]

Buddhist Contemplative Practice

Even though Buddhism is not *just* meditation, its contemplative tradition is rich and has been preserved by generations of Buddhists to the present day. This treasure is now unfolding in the West, where different schools, traditions, and practices of Buddhism are coming together for the first time, though this potpourri of languages, teachings, and practices can be confusing, even for dedicated Buddhists.

This book draws on the contemplative practices of various Buddhist schools as practical resources to help with the journey of aging. I have tried to keep them simple, and limited them to four types: mindfulness of body and breath; compassion and gratitude; transforming emotions; and spacious awareness. Each of these types has a particular flavor, purpose, and meaning.

MINDFULNESS OF BODY AND BREATH

"Mindfulness" in a Buddhist sense means "concentrated nonjudgmental attention to what is happening." Mindfulness is a particular way of paying attention. While we can be mindful of any experience—physical, mental, or emotional—mindfulness of body and breath is foundational. Buddhist contemplative practice is rooted in the body.

We usually have no trouble paying attention to the things we like or enjoy; we can be quite focused in the pursuit of love, money, power, and other things that we want. Mindfulness means paying attention whether we like it or not, without judgment or interpretation. Mindfulness trains us to accept our experience just as it is.

The physical body is the most insistent bellweather of our aging, and most people in the second half of life are paying close attention to the body in terms of stamina, vigor, skin care, diet, weight loss, and attractiveness. But how many of us pay attention to our bodies *without judgment*? How many of us actually experience our bodies just as they are?

Aging Breath by Breath in Chapter 2 and vertical time in Chapter 5 are examples of mindful awareness as applied to the aging body. As far as our bodies are concerned, aging tends to happen faster and cause more trouble for us when we aren't aware of it. When we fail to notice that our lower back is a little stiff when we get up in the morning, we are more likely to really injure it later in the day. The same applies to mental and emotional injuries; they start small, but if we neglect them, soon they become larger.

COMPASSION AND GRATITUDE

Compassion begins as a kind of mindfulness. We train ourselves to notice our own and other people's feelings and try to sustain that awareness. But compassion as a contemplative practice goes beyond mindfulness. Compassion is proactive. We actively work to generate and strengthen compassionate feelings, both in meditation and in daily life. We need to do this work because we do not start life as fully developed compassionate beings. In fact, as young children, we are self-centered and focused on our own needs. It is only when we begin to understand that other people have needs, too, that compassion dawns.

Even as adults some part of us still expresses that needy, self-centered child, especially when we are fearful, anxious, or depressed. That child can also reemerge when we are feeling overwhelmed by the challenges of growing old. As Buddhists, we cultivate compassion whenever we can. The Loving Kindness Prayer at the conclusion of this chapter, as well as the Sending and Receiving contemplation of Chapter 9, are both examples of traditional compassion practices. The gratitude reflections of Chapter 4 are closely related.

Compassion and gratitude can arise out of mutual connectedness. Compassion and gratitude are like a daily tonic that can lift our spirits. But they are much more than medicine. They are fundamental principles or qualities of all life. When I was young, I attended Sunday school, where we often sang the song "God Is Love." I liked the song, though as an eight-year-old, I couldn't say why. Now, as I look back to that feeling, I realize that the truth of it was clear to me. Love is the highest form of connectedness. Even as a child, I understood that.

The natural spiritual intelligence we have as children never leaves us. It is deep inside, waiting to be called forth. Compassion practices are like this. They draw their power from what we already know. Compassion and kindness, when directed back toward ourselves, help us tolerate our own aging and the aging of those around us. Due to the aftereffects of both illness and age, I tend to knock things over—such as glasses of water—more than I used to, and when I do, I tend to be hard on myself. "Stupid!" I scold myself.

"Don't say that," my wife gently reminds me. "You're not stupid. You're just a little slower than you used to be."

And then I remember: I must be kind to myself and kind to others as well. There's nothing wrong with being a little slower.

INSIGHT

Contemplative practice is nourished by two essential foods: focus and insight. Without focus we cannot see clearly, and without insight, focus doesn't really change us. Everyone can be focused when they want something. In Chapter 1, Ikkyu's wealthy patron was focused on getting a scroll to impress his friends, and Ikkyu was focused on teaching the patron a lesson.

Without focus, meditation devolves into reverie and daydreaming. But meditative focus alone is not transformative. Focus in meditation is like a lens or a magnifying glass. It allows us to see our experience more clearly. That is good, but now that we can see better, what is the wisdom that seeing our experience brings to us?

Behind all Buddhist contemplative practice is the conviction that we can grow, we can change—and not just when we are young, but throughout our lives. Until fairly recently, brain scientists thought that we are born with a fixed number of brain cells and could not grow any more. New imaging techniques and the discovery of "brain plasticity" has corrected that misperception. The brain creates new neurons all the time and in response to injury creates huge numbers of them.

When I was in rehabilitation after a brain infection, my doctor told me a story about brain plasticity. She said that when mice were taught to run through a maze to find cheese and were later examined, they had grown many new brain neurons. But when they had to *swim* through water too deep to stand in to find the cheese, the number of new neurons was enormous.

This kind of result has transformed rehabilitation medicine and is instructive for spiritual practice as well. Through the insight gained in spiritual practice, we can change, and when we are facing great challenges, our change can be even greater. In other words, Buddhist meditation is not just about being relaxed and calm, but about seeing through our problems and difficulties to find a new way. Just as the mice in the maze found a way to the cheese—even under great difficulty—through contemplative reflection we can find our way to new possibilities and solutions to problems.

SPACIOUS AWARENESS

The relationship between focus and insight in meditation can also be expressed as a balance between effort and surrender.

Jim, a retreat participant, complained after a meditation session that he was having a hard time keeping track of his breath. "I'm too busy thinking about whether I'm going to get the job I just applied for."

I advised him not to try so hard and just relax.

"If I relax, I fall asleep," he replied.

I told him that was OK too. Eventually, I told him, you'll wake up.

The effort to focus can be hard, especially for beginners. In Buddhism, the distracted mind is often likened to a monkey, jumping from here to there, while the focused mind is pictured as an elephant: calm, steady, and deliberate. The balanced state of meditation is sometimes pictured as a monkey riding on top of an elephant.

Beyond the efforts of monkey and elephant, there is another kind of contemplative practice that is more like surrender. It goes by many names. In the Zen tradition we say "just sitting" or "just awareness." Tibetan Buddhism speaks of "resting in true nature." When I am speaking in an interfaith context, I might use the term "the prayer of silence" or "divine presence." This awareness is called "spacious" because it feels like a clear blue sky or a boundless ocean. It is called "awareness" because it is not focused on anything in particular; it is just awake and conscious.

In Buddhism, simply resting in a relaxed, open, spacious state of mind without purpose and without a goal is considered the highest form of spiritual practice, and all of Chapter 10 is devoted to it. If the distracted mind is like a monkey, and the calm mind is like an elephant, "just awareness" practice might be thought of as an all-encompassing radiance that includes monkey, elephant, ourselves, and everything else.

This spacious awareness is considered both an advanced practice and a practice even the merest beginner can do. This seems to be paradoxical, but when a beginner does it, it has the quality and substance of a beginner's awareness, and when an advanced meditator does it, it has a deeper quality of advanced awareness.

That is why I like to call it a prayer of silence. Prayer is not really something you get "good" at, like other skills—although people who pray regularly have cultivated a prayerful attitude toward life. A prayer is in essence a surrender and a supplication to that which is beyond ourselves. In this sense the Buddhist practice of spacious awareness has a universality that makes it kindred with other religions.

The Loving Kindness Prayer

The prayer and contemplation on Loving Kindness has become one of the most popular Buddhist practices being taught in the West. It has its roots in the Loving Kindness or "Metta" Scripture taught by the Buddha. This short hymn to compassion exhorts us to "cherish all living things."

> Even as a mother at the risk of her life watches over and protects her only child, so with a boundless mind should one cherish all living things, suffusing love over the entire world, above, below, and all around without limit; so let one cultivate an infinite goodwill toward the whole world.

In my own spiritual communities, we recite the following verse from the Loving Kindness Scripture after every meditation session:

> *May I be filled with loving kindness;*
> *May I be free from suffering;*
> *May I be happy and at peace.*

We say it three times beginning "May *I*...," three times beginning "May *we*...," and three times beginning "May *all beings*...,"—nine times in all. That way it includes everyone, including each person in the room.

This recitation is a kind of aspirational prayer. We know

that not all people, including ourselves, are always filled with loving kindness. We know that they are not free from suffering, nor are they always happy and at peace.

But we wish for loving kindness nevertheless. Skeptics may say that wishing won't help. If we want to improve the world's happiness, they say, we have to actually *do* something. This prayer does not exclude *doing* something in an activist sense. All of Chapter 9, Giving Back, is devoted to that kind of activity.

But reciting this prayer helps in one way: It changes the hearts of those reciting it. And when I change, everyone I know and meet is changed by seeing the change in me. And so it is for those people too; everyone who knows them is changed. It is a little like a spiritual chain letter, or, in the parlance of the online world, like a YouTube video going viral.

I once heard of a church in Russia where a hermit lived fifty feet underground in a cell beneath the altar. No one who visited the church ever saw the hermit or spoke to him; in fact he had taken a vow of silence. But they knew he was there. Because of the hermit, the church became famous for its holiness. People came from far and wide just to be near the hermit and feel his blessing.

This is the power of prayer. When I was in a coma and near death due to my encephalitis, the word went out in many Buddhist communities that I might be dying. These communities included me in their daily chants and recitations. They recited the Loving Kindness prayer for me. My coma was so deep that I had no awareness of the outside world. Even when doctors shined a light into my eyes, my pupils did not react. That was a dire symptom.

Nevertheless, inside my coma I was having many visions. In one I remember sitting with a group of people on bales of hay in a barn. It was late summer, and the smell of the hay was sweet. Some of the people were my Buddhist friends; some I did not know. We were passing around a hot drink, perhaps tea or broth, and engaging in friendly conversation. Every so often the group would chant or sing something. It was a pleasant, friendly sound.

I felt safe there, and knew I would be taken care of. My friends were with me.

Two weeks later I woke up.

Contemplative Reflection

THE LOVING KINDNESS PRAYER

There are many forms of the Loving Kindness prayer. Some Buddhist teachers hold retreats where participants repeat the prayer in silence to themselves for hours or days. Profound experiences can occur. This prayer is suitable for every circumstance—for people who are dying as well as those who are healthy, for those young as well as old, for people in pain and suffering and people who feel quite content. Thus it can be a useful resource for us as we age. Whatever our circumstance, whatever our age or state of health, we can wish happiness for ourselves and for others.

This is the version of the Loving Kindness prayer I recommend for aging well:

> *As I grow older, may I be kind to myself;*
> *As I grow older, may I accept joy and sorrow;*
> *As I grow older, may I be happy and at peace.*

Say it a few times to yourself, just to get the feeling of it. When I do it, I feel the same way as I did long ago in that barn of my dream state: friendly, relaxed, taken care of. All compassion practices in Buddhism first begin by being directed at oneself. Until we can generate compassion for the precious person we know best, it is hard to truly share it with others.

Now say it this way:

> *As each of us grows older, may we be kind to ourselves;*
> *As each of us grows older, may we accept joy and sorrow;*
> *As each of us grows older, may we be happy and at peace.*

Now we are sharing this wish not just for ourselves, but for spouses, partners, family, friends—all those who are with us on the aging journey. It is not ever a journey that we take alone. Everyone we know is with us.

Lastly, say it this way:

> *As all beings grow older, may they be kind to themselves;*

As all beings grow older, may they accept joy and
  sorrow;
As all beings grow older, may they be happy and at
  peace.

Now we have expanded our prayer to embrace all people everywhere. Whatever joys and sorrows accompany our aging, they belong not just to us or the people we know, but to everyone. All humanity walks together on this journey. The expedition is timeless; we have always been doing it.

You can recite this prayer when you wake up in the morning, anytime during the day, and when you go to bed at night. You can use the traditional version ("May I be filled with loving kindness . . .") or the aging version ("As I grow older, may I be kind to myself . . .") or both.

Sometimes in my congregations, after we have finished reciting the Loving Kindness prayer for ourselves, for each other, and for all beings, I say, "May it be so."

You can do this too. After you have finished the prayer, add, "May it be so."

Whether the wishes of the prayer are true in any worldly, objective sense, it is true that you have said them and mean them.

The prayer is true because you are true.

CHAPTER 8

Conquering the
Five Fears

Recently I was having dinner with a good friend of mine, a physician still practicing at age seventy-nine. "I've lived a great life, Lew," he told me. "I have children, grandchildren, a rewarding profession—everything anyone could want. Not much scares me, except for one thing—Alzheimer's. I'm terrified of that. I'd rather drop dead of a heart attack."

As I listened to him, I reflected on how older people have many fears that younger people haven't even begun to think about. Then I remembered a teaching from the ancient Buddhist tradition called the "five great fears": fear of death, fear of illness, fear of losing one's mind, fear of loss of livelihood, and fear of public speaking. Except for the last, these great fears seem to describe the very kinds of anxiety—like my friend's fear of Alzheimer's—that aging brings.

For a while I wondered why the fifth fear—fear of public

speaking—was included with these other life-threatening issues. Finally I came to realize that this fifth fear was actually a clue to the other four. Those who have a fear of public speaking can have paralyzing anxiety. One woman who suffered from it said to me, "Lew, to be honest I'd rather slit my throat than speak in front of a crowd."

Then I understood. These five fears are called "great" because each of them can cause panic and trigger the autonomic nervous system. The prospect of death, illness, losing one's mind, losing one's livelihood—and yes, even speaking in front of a crowd—can cause panic. The ancient Buddhists classified these fears together because they all affect the nervous system in the same way.

I myself enjoy speaking to large groups of people, but I have plenty of experience with the other four fears, as do many of my acquaintances. Each of them has a story to tell.

Fear of Death. A friend of mine traveling in Europe stepped out of the elevator in his hotel and began to feel faint. He had only a moment to feel a rising panic and think, "This could be it," before he lost consciousness. He awoke on the floor a few seconds later to find a maid bending over him. He said a quick prayer of thanks and waited until his heart stopped pounding. Later, a doctor said he was dehydrated. He was relieved, but he also knew he had stepped to the edge of the cliff and looked over. He had faced the first fear: fear of dying.

Fear of Illness. One morning a few years ago, I awoke feeling feverish. I took my temperature; it was 102. I took it again an hour later and it read 103. By noon it was almost 104, and on the advice of my doctor, I was on the way to the hospital. I felt a rising panic. I'd had so much illness in my life! Not again, I thought.

It turned out to be nothing serious, just a flu. But for a short time the fear of illness overwhelmed me. It wasn't rational. It was the memory of all those other times that triggered the panic response.

Fear of Losing One's Mind. Any time people over sixty can't think of a word or name, or wonder where they left their glasses, the thought of Alzheimer's rears its head; they joke about it as a "senior moment," but fear lurks beneath the humor. Many older people go for regular neurological testing to keep one step ahead of this fear, but the testing can cause fear too. One man who had flown bombers during the Korean War told me he was more afraid of the testing than he had been the bombing missions. "On a mission," he said, "you either came back or you didn't. With these tests . . ." He didn't finish his sentence.

Fear of Loss of Livelihood. In the past few years, this fear has reemerged in a way that only the oldest living Americans still remember: Back in the 1930s people who lost their jobs sometimes jumped out of windows. Today, polls show that most Americans who have not lost a job themselves know people who have. Nest eggs have shrunk; once secure plans for retirement have vanished. This fear is particularly daunting for older Americans, who must compete with younger workers in the job market, have a sense that they are running out of time, and harbor a general feeling of helplessness. Even for vigorous middle-aged people who have not yet had to face health worries, livelihood anxiety can keep them awake at night.

Fear of Public Speaking. Another friend told me about the time she spoke to an audience of two thousand professional colleagues. She stood up, forced a grin, and began, "I want you all to know I'm absolutely terrified. So I want you all to smile."

Everyone laughed. The laughter broke the ice and she was able to get through her talk—barely.

"I'm highly intelligent, well respected in my field, and competent in so many ways," she told me later. "It's so embarrassing to go through this time after time."

I told her about the five great fears and she was somewhat mollified. "At least the Buddhists weren't too embarrassed to mention it," she said.

Coping Strategies. The point of all these stories is that fear is a regular part of life, and certain fears are particular to the second half of life. The only compensating factor is that by the time we are over fifty we have a lot of practice! Facing our fears is one part of coping, but so is denial and compartmentalization. One psychiatrist I know calls denial a real blessing. "Without it," he says, "we probably couldn't survive what life throws at us."

Some people are born with an unusual capacity for

denial; they seem to have a knack for ignoring their problems. Low-denial types, in contrast, use worry as their way of mastering their problems, or at least addressing them.

And in addition to high and low denial, there is a one more coping strategy, which I call "non-denial." This is what in the Buddhist tradition we would term "mindfulness." Mindfulness means to pay close attention to what is actually happening. As a strategy for dealing with fear, it operates somewhat outside of the nexus of high and low denial.

High Denial

Until recently the exact mechanisms of denial were not well understood. In the classic Freudian view, denial was seen as a psychological and sometimes neurotic process. But recent research shows that the process of denial is mostly neurological; the brain actually alters neural pathways so as to make unpleasant thoughts and memories inaccessible. It makes sense that this capacity would have evolved to help us deal with difficulty. Without it, we might be so overwhelmed with sadness or anxiety that we couldn't function.

We all know people who seem especially good at this. I once knew a policeman named Bill who supervised patrol cars at night in the most dangerous neighborhoods. He often heard gunfire and had been shot at many times. I asked him whether he was ever afraid and he said, "No. Not really. You just do the job." High denial helped Bill. Someone who worried more wouldn't be able to do what he did.

In other circumstances, denial can be disastrous. Robert,

a freelance writer, was an alcoholic. He had had a couple of DUIs but somehow was still driving. All his friends, including myself, tried everything to get him into a program, or at least to admit his problem, but nothing worked. "Forget it, man," he would say. "I'm in control."

One night I got a call from a mutual friend. Robert had wrapped his car around a telephone pole and was killed instantly. In the next hours, as his friends traded telephone calls and shared the news, we all thought and said the same thing: "If only there were something we could have done."

A different example of high denial was Roland, who had an upcoming presentation to make at work, one that would determine whether the department he headed would continue to receive funding. His job was on the line. When the day came, he walked into the kitchen for breakfast, and his wife—who for weeks had been so worried she barely slept—asked him if he was ready for the big day.

"What big day?" Roland said with complete innocence. He had forgotten.

A psychiatrist told me this story, which he had heard from Roland's wife.

"You're kidding!" I said. "People can have that level of denial?"

"You'd be amazed," the psychiatrist said.

On the surface, high denial seems to provide those who do it with equanimity and calm in the face of threat or danger. Sometimes, as in the case of Bill, it can serve them well. Other times, as in Robert's and Roland's cases, it can be counterproductive or even dangerous.

Low Denial

Low denial people are life's chronic worriers. Judy, a breast cancer survivor, described to me how this worked for her. "I try to think of the worst possible scenario," she explained. "And then I imagine dealing with it. I figure if I can deal with the worst, I can deal with anything short of that. I do that every day."

Low denial has its advantages. In some ways it is more realistic. Judy had a much better grasp of her problem than Roland did. Low denial people face their fears and strategize how to deal with them. But "thinking of the worst possible scenario" has a cost. Judy acknowledged that she was seeing a therapist for stress and was taking antianxiety medication.

Judy and Roland would have difficulty understanding each other's coping strategies. A high denial person like Roland might look at Judy's situation and think, "Why is she making all that fuss? I'd wait and deal with the cancer if it came back." And while a person's capacity for denial is somewhat innate—Judy and Roland had probably always coped that way—to some extent denial can be learned or unlearned as a developing skill. The skill-based aspect of denial, particularly when it involves moment-by-moment worries, is called "compartmentalization." Compartmentalization is something that can be adjusted and practiced. Low denial people can learn to compartmentalize more, and high denial people can learn how to compartmentalize less.

Compartmentalization

Compartmentalization is the mental faculty that keeps us focused on the task at hand and allows distracting thoughts and anxieties to recede into the unconscious. Compartmentalization is the moment-to-moment functioning of denial. Usually this process happens without our thinking about it. We may go off to work knowing that our six-year-old has the chicken pox, and we certainly think about it, but the thought doesn't prevent us from doing our work. It also doesn't show; we can carry on a cogent conversation with a coworker without suddenly staring off into space thinking about the chicken pox. Conversely, we are not so detached from the thought of our sick child that we forget to call the babysitter who is staying at home with him. This is normal compartmentalization.

However, when it comes to the "great" fears, our ability to compartmentalize can veer out of the normal range and our compartmentalization can become either too weak or too strong. I had that experience when I emerged from an encephalitic coma with brain damage, and my brain seemed to have completely lost the ability to compartmentalize. I was obsessed with all sorts of worries. Suppose I never recovered the ability to do computer programming? I'd have no livelihood! Suppose the encephalitis came back? I would die! Suppose my wife became ill? Or died? There'd be no one to take care of me! These worries plagued me to the extent that some days they were nearly all I could talk or think about.

Francesca, my therapist at that time, understood that I was suffering from "disinhibitory syndrome"—a common symptom of brain injury—and worked with me on a technique to strengthen my compartmentalization. When compartmentalization is weak, she explained, the mind can't keep the worry safely tucked away in the unconscious, and it keeps intruding.

"When you find you can't set your worry aside, tell yourself you're not going to think about it now. You'll think about it later," she said. "Then pick a time in the future when you'll take up the worry. Promise yourself that when the time comes you'll be able to worry all you want. Until then, whenever the worry comes back, remind yourself it's not time yet." Francesca advised me to start small. At first, she said, pick a time ten or fifteen minutes in the future. She encouraged me to set a timer or an alarm.

At first even fifteen minutes was too much. It was humiliating to realize how little control I had over my thoughts— I, a trained Buddhist meditator! When I confessed this to Francesca, she laughed. "Even trained Buddhist meditators can have a brain injury," she said.

Little by little—ten, fifteen, or twenty minutes at a time—I held my worries at bay. It helped to pick a word or phrase to say in place of my worries. The best one was the time I had picked to start worrying again. "Ten thirty," I would whisper to myself. "Can't worry until ten thirty!"

I would also imagine the door of a bank vault closing on my worries whenever I said, "Ten thirty." It was interesting to discover that when ten thirty came, the worry was weaker. Training my mind to hold off worrying, even for a little while, took the circular or amplifying quality out of the worry.

"I do this exercise myself," Francesca said. "Otherwise I'd be thinking about my patients all night."

In contrast, people whose compartmentalization is too strong need to go in the opposite direction. Their problem is that they are too good at keeping their worries and problems at bay—so good that they may not even be aware they have problems. They need to invite their problems and their worry into consciousness. Not having any experience of this myself, I asked Francesca how she dealt with people who compartmentalize too much.

She said that she asks them to think of one or two big problems in their life, and then agree to think about them for a set period of time, such as fifteen minutes. "At first they don't like it," she said. "They come up with all kinds of excuses. But I have them stick with it. Eventually they do it and are amazed to find that they actually have problems. They somehow had convinced themselves they were problem-free."

Non-Denial

In addition to all these approaches, Buddhism offers a third way: a practice I call "non-denial." Non-denial is really just mindfulness, in other words, paying nonjudgmental attention to what is happening now. In this kind of mindful awareness we neither take up the worry nor try to push it away. We just observe it.

Dr. Jon Kabat-Zinn discovered this application of mindfulness when he first used it as a method for treating chronic pain. Pain, like anxiety or fear, is deeply unpleasant and our natural reaction is to run away from it. Dr. Kabat-Zinn had his patients resist that temptation; instead, he had them just observe the pain. Paradoxically, this approach made the pain more bearable. What he learned is that fear, like physical pain, is unpleasant, but unlike physical pain, it is a mixture of many things: bodily sensations, memories, imagined futures, visualizations, and looping and repetitive inner dialogues. Part of what makes fear difficult to manage is that it is so complex and multifaceted. Mindfulness can separate it into its separate parts and make it more manageable.

This is the method I used the day I had the high fever. First there were all the bodily sensations of fever: chills, muscle aches, and fatigue. When I took my temperature, to these bodily sensations was added an objective fact: 102 on the thermometer. Just these facts themselves were alarming.

Now unpleasant memories came flooding in. Years before, I had taken my temperature over hours and days and watched it steadily climb—100, 101, 102, 103. I became nauseated and finally so dizzy I couldn't stand. Just in time, I went to the emergency room and within hours was in an encephalitic coma. An hour or two more and I would have died. Now it was all happening again; my fever was climbing, and all those old memories were returning. Every alarm bell was ringing now.

But it wasn't happening again. The encephalitis was years ago. Now I was fully recovered and healthy. Healthy people get fevers too, and not necessarily from encephalitis. I watched my symptoms closely and realized that in fact they were not the same. There were important differences. I was not suffering from severe vertigo, I did not have a loud roaring in my ears, and I could think clearly. I was still afraid, but I had a handle on my fear.

When the fever reached 104 I called my doctor. He was aware of my medical history and he said, "Go to the emergency room now!" It was déjà vu for both of us. I put on a heavy jacket, walked to the car, and got in on the passenger side. My wife drove, my heart raced, and we pulled up to the same emergency room door as we had that night long ago.

Except this time it was not midnight; it was the middle of the afternoon. Unlike the last time, I was lucid and coherent. I wasn't disoriented or dizzy; I could walk. Again I talked to my fear. "This is like the last time," I said. "But it isn't the same. This is different."

This is different. I kept telling myself that as we walked into the emergency room, with its same sights and smells, its same layout—even some of the same nurses.

This is different. Even though I was put on a gurney, admitted to the hospital, and wheeled up to a room, I kept practicing mindful attention, paying attention to *exactly* what was happening as well as what was *not* happening.

I was afraid of illness; I was afraid of dying. I was afraid that once again I might lose everything. But fear is less than the sum of its parts. Pay attention to the parts and fear loses some of its sting.

"This isn't so bad," I said to Amy as I lay down in my new hospital bed and as nurses and doctors scurried in and out. At this point, with their eye on my thick folder of medical history, I think they were more worried than I was.

"I'm OK," I said to her.

And I was.

Inner Dialogue

My father, a self-educated, introspective man, came to the dinner table one evening and said, "You can't stop thinking. It's always going on."

He said this as though he had figured out something important. I was eight years old at the time and didn't have any idea what he was talking about. But I remembered the comment, and when I began to investigate meditation ten years later, I realized that my father was half-right. Our inner dialogue does go on, mostly unconsciously, but it can be changed, and even stopped. That is one of the things meditation can do.

Inner dialogue, which is sometimes referred to as "stream of consciousness," is primarily verbal and is usually random, a running inner commentary on the events of the moment. In contrast, worry, fear, and anxiety produce an inner dialogue that is not random. The same sequence of thoughts repeats over and over. We rehearse scenarios in our head: What will he or she say? What will I say? Suppose this; suppose that. As we have seen, compartmentalization can break the loop, but when the worry is too intense, it can overwhelm compartmental barriers, and stronger medicine is needed.

"Calm Lake" is a focused visualization that reduces the energy and repetitiveness of worry. It replaces the words of inner dialogue with an image—that of a lake—and uses feedback to replace the "bad weather" of worry with the "good weather" of calm.

Contemplative Reflection

CALM LAKE

This reflection is best done in a meditation posture, sitting in a chair or on a cushion. But I have also had good success doing it while sitting in a doctor's waiting room or in an airport lounge. It is good medicine for agitation or worry, but it can be done as a regular practice regardless of your state of mind. Some members of my meditation group like it better than breath meditation. They like the fact that it is visual.

Begin by picturing or imagining a small lake. It helps if you can remember a real lake that you once visited. It should be small enough so that you can see the whole outline of the shore. Fill in the surroundings with imagined detail. Imagine that the shore is lined with maple and oak. Let them be the green of spring, or the brilliant yellows and reds of fall.

If you are imagining the lake scene, it usually helps to do so with your eyes closed. Another method is to select a postcard or small photograph of a lake scene and put it in front of you. If you do this, look at it with half-closed eyes and a soft gaze, at least until the scene is vivid in your mind's eye. Enter the scene and imagine yourself sitting lakeside, gazing out over the water.

The water represents your state of mind, so take a moment to tune in to your state. If you are doing the Calm Lake meditation because you are worried, agitated, or anxious, there will be "waves" both in your mind and on the lake. Scan your body to see how this agitation feels physically. Butterflies in the stomach, tightness in the chest, and constriction in the throat are all physical signs of tension and stress.

Now return to your image of the lake and picture the "weather" there as a reflection of your state of mind. If your thoughts are agitated and choppy, picture the water as agitated and choppy. If your mood is dark and cloudy, picture the sky as dark and cloudy. Just watch the weather from the lakeshore as a disinterested observer. Let the weather develop its own visual details. Perhaps the trees on the opposite shore are waving ominously in the wind. Perhaps the water near your feet is hitting the shore with noisy lapping. Fill in the whole scene with as much detail as possible.

Now imagine that you have some magic power over the weather on the lake, so that merely by wishing it to be, you can gradually calm the weather down. Little by little the surface of the lake becomes less agitated and more smooth.

Its condition may go back and forth for a while. You may feel the lake growing calmer, and then it may kick up again, reflecting a new burst of mental agitation. Be patient; soothe the surface of the lake and the weather around it with kindness and patience. In the end, it is your image, your lake. It can be what you want it to be.

As you continue to relax into the calm waters of the lake, how do you feel now? Spend a few moments tuning in to the changing feeling in your body. How do your arms feel now? Your skin? Your face? And how does your breath feel as you rest your gaze on the now-glassy surface of the calm lake? Include that feeling in your awareness and let it fill your whole body.

Now think of your breath as helping you maintain your focus. Let your breath flow naturally in and out without pressure or strain. Let it be delicate and quiet. Think of your breath as mirroring and reflecting the glassy smooth surface of the lake. You want to breathe smoothly so as not to ruffle the waters.

Gradually let your attention shift, focusing less on the image of the calm lake, and more on this feeling of your breath, letting the feeling of the lake merge into the feeling of your breath. Your breathing has now absorbed the feeling of the calm lake. Let that feeling abide and continue in your body and breathing. Remain that way for as long as you feel comfortable.

This is the essence of the Calm Lake meditation. It takes a while to describe it, but doing it is smooth and quick.

To review, it has three stages. In the first stage, either looking at a picture with open eyes or imagining the scene with eyes closed, you establish the image of the lake and gradually see the lake as smooth and calm. In the second stage, you adjust your breathing to mirror the calm feeling of the lake. In the third, you let the image of the lake fade and melt into your relaxed, smooth breathing. Your breathing becomes the lake; your mind becomes the breathing.

Some people find the image of a calm lake immediately soothing and natural; others have more difficulty connecting to it. As an alternative to a lake, you can also picture a mountain—solid, snow-capped and massively still against a clear blue sky. If you use a mountain image, you may want to replace the surface of the lake as a representation of your state of mind with an image of snow on the mountain swirling in the wind. As your mind calms, the wind dies down, the snow settles, and the image of the mountain becomes sharp and clear.

With either image, the point is to picture expansiveness and stillness, and by holding your attention on that picture, absorb that stillness into your own body.

Through this meditation we transform the horizontal stream of our inner dialogue into a single, stable moment, renewing itself on each breath. Done regularly, especially when you are agitated or upset, even five or ten minutes of this meditation can offer great benefit. And even when you are not upset, Calm Lake is a wonderful centering exercise for daily living.

CHAPTER 9

Giving Back

I was a college student in Boston during the 1965 blackout that plunged the whole eastern seaboard into darkness. No one knew what was happening, and everyone was frightened. Standing at the bus stop in the pitch dark, I got on a dimly lit trolley to go home. It was still running because Boston had a stand-alone electrical system that powered its trolleys. As the driver took my money, he said, "They're here."

I asked him what he meant.

"The power is out from the Canadian border to Washington, D.C. Who could do that? It's the flying-saucer people. It has to be. Yep, they're here." He was calm as he kept driving.

All over Boston, citizens grabbed flashlights and ran into the street to direct traffic. Bars and restaurants handed out candles. The population of the entire city joined hands and became one. This is what human beings always do in a crisis or common threat. It is built into our nature. During Hurricane Katrina, the tsunamis in Southeast Asia and Japan, the earthquakes in Haiti, New Zealand, and Japan—just to name a few crises that happened during the writing of this book—the story was the same. Individuals set aside their differences and joined together to help.

In other words, we are programmed to help each other, and when the need is great, that quality emerges strongly and overrides individual needs and concern. This principle probably unites religions around the world more than any other.

To help others when they are in need is so natural that we rarely stop to think about the full scope of its benefits. Helping others brings out the best in us at any age, but as we grow older, helping takes on an additional coloration and value. We begin to experience it more not just as helping, but as "giving back." As life progresses into middle and old age, we come to feel that this life is a gift that we yearn to repay.

Aging research has shown that this giving back is not just beneficial to others; it is good for us, too. A 2003 study[17] concluded, "Programs designed to help [older] people feel supported may need to be redesigned so that the emphasis is on what people do to help others."

While the research tells us that helping others helps us in various ways, it doesn't say exactly how. What specifically happens psychologically, physically, and emotionally when acts of generosity are performed? How does each party benefit? And what are the qualities that make it so positive for healthy aging?

To find out, I talked to several people in middle age who were deeply engaged in giving back. One was volunteering to teach meditation in a women's prison, another was part of a medical team volunteering in India and Burma, and a third had been a clinical psychologist who volunteered to help the homeless.

Among the questions I asked each of them were: Why are you doing the work you do? How has it changed you? What has inspired you? And finally, What are you doing to take care of yourself?

Connection

Susan had been teaching meditation in a women's prison for many years. When I asked her why she was doing this work, she first reflected on her status as a privileged person in society. She felt the need to "plow back" the gifts she had received to those less fortunate, and meditation was something she could offer. When I pointed out that she was also an older woman and that most of the women she worked with in the prison were in their twenties and thirties, she nodded. "They're my own daughter's age," she said. "In some ways for these young women in prison, I'm like their mom."

How had the experienced changed her? She replied that it made her feel more connected with the world as it really is. "It's connection," she said. "That's what sustains me. That's my food." She went on to tell me about one young woman, new to the prison, who had come to the meditation group for the first time, and all during the meditation did nothing but cry. When it came her turn to share what the experience had been for her, this woman said through tears how much she missed her young daughter. Susan asked her if there was anything she or the women there could do to help. "You already have," the woman said. "You are all here with me. I don't feel so alone anymore."

Mark, having stepped down as the director of an international nonprofit, was now devoting himself to the plight of poor people in Bangladesh and Burma. Although he had just turned sixty and had various health problems, he still traveled to Asia several times a year.

Given such a taxing schedule for someone his age, I asked what he did to take care of himself.

"I don't really worry about it," he replied. "I feel this is what I have to do, and I figure one way or another, things will work out. Nevertheless, I watch what I eat and drink when I travel, and I schedule a week or two of rest and relaxation when I get back."

Mark explained that, like Susan, he had a sense of wanting to "balance the scales" between the affluence of his own country and the grinding poverty and oppression of the countries he worked in. He also felt that his charitable work helped sustain and deepen meditation practice and spiritual vows. "Gary Snyder once wrote an essay about engagement in the world," Mark said. "In it he wrote that the mercy of the West is social justice, and the mercy of the East is insight into the nature of the self. We need both, I think, and I see my work as a way to bridge those two aspects. Besides, it keeps me young. I'm like a kid in school, learning something new every day. Physically I may be slowing down, but mentally I'm still on the way up. That's how I feel."

Mark then told me this story: Once, while on a visit to rural Bangladesh, he stood in the fields at sunset watching the men come back to the village from work. "As they walked back, they were all holding hands," Mark said. "They owned virtually nothing, they were the poorest of the poor, but they had each other, and they were holding hands as they walked through the fields. I can't tell you how deeply that moved me. Just seeing them made my work worthwhile. Now that I'm getting old, I can't do what I used to, but I'm connected to all these struggling people and they're connected to each other. I hear people say that I'm giving back. But when I saw those men, I felt them giving back to me."

Dr. Russell, a psychiatrist who treats primarily older patients, confirmed the value of giving back. He says that the people who do best with aging are those who actively seek a helping role, as Susan and Mark have done. It is common, Dr. Russell said, for such people to take up helping activities related to their earlier work or career. A retired doctor might volunteer at a local health clinic. A historian, politician, or economist might volunteer as a teacher. An accountant might volunteer to do bookkeeping for the local chapter of the Red Cross.

But Dr. Russell also included a caveat: It's not healthy for older people to give back in a one-sided way. They also have to take care of themselves. "The people I see who really do well with their aging are the ones who divide their time between actively helping others and doing things that are just for them," Dr. Russell said, "things that give them enjoyment and pleasure. You've got to put something in both baskets—giving to others and giving to yourself. You have to find that balance."

Inspiration

After a long career as a clinical psychologist in private practice, Eric—the third person I consulted on the effects of giving back—cut back his billable hours and volunteered as a case worker in a clinic for homeless people. "Private practice was all right, and it paid well, but after doing it for so long I thought to myself, I want to work with *real* problems. Of course my clients' problems were real enough. But my work just didn't inspire me the way it used to when I was young."

From day one, Eric got what he wished for. The problems of his new clients were utterly basic. If someone was hungry, Eric got them food. If they needed a place to sleep, he found them a place. It was extremely tough, Eric told me, seeing people day after day who were desperate, with absolutely nothing. But over time he found that whenever he could restore some small piece of their human dignity, it was truly inspiring. "Here's a true story," Eric said.

> I was walking down the street one day and this well-dressed young man on a bicycle with a briefcase pulled up next to me and said, "Eric! Remember me? I'm Bruce. You pulled me out of the gutter when I was drop-dead drunk, and you said to me, 'You can beat this; I know you can.' And I heard you, and I got myself into rehab, and I did beat it. Look at me now. I've got a job and an apartment and a girlfriend. I've even got stock options! All because of you. Thanks, man."
>
> There's nothing like that feeling. The work in the clinic was incredibly difficult, and sometimes I'd come home at night and wonder what I'd gotten myself into. But then you run into somebody like Bruce and you realize why you do it. In private practice, I knew that I was helping. But on the street, I wasn't just helping; I was literally saving lives. I had my life, but those street people didn't. It was like mouth-to-mouth resuscitation.

When I asked Eric what was the deepest lesson he learned serving the homeless, he said, "Human beings have incredible courage. You can't believe how much they have. People get up in the morning wherever they are—behind a Dumpster or in a doorway—and keep on hoping. I was in awe of these people."

Giving back and sharing what we have, especially when we are older and have so much to give, is transformative as well as inspiring. The scientific research that says giving back is good for our health is true enough, but it isn't the whole story. The human spirit, so full of heart, is unquenchable. To whatever extent we can engage with it, it nourishes us at every level: physically, emotionally, and spiritually.

Contemplative Reflections

SENDING AND RECEIVING

In the Buddhist tradition, the "perfection of giving" is one of the primary virtues of an enlightened person. For Buddhists, giving back is outwardly expressed as service to others, and inwardly expressed in training the mind to cultivate a generous spirit. This principle is central to the Buddhist vision of the spiritual life, and it is expressed in various ways.

Long ago, Buddhist meditation teachers developed a method for strengthening the mind's capacity for generosity. Once this practice was the exclusive preserve of yogis, yoginis, monks, and nuns, but more recently it has been widely taught and practiced in the West.

The practice of "Sending and Receiving compassion," often just called "Sending and Receiving," builds on the mind's natural capacity to visualize or imagine, together with our innate desire to connect and give back. This visualization can be turned to ourselves as well as to others—a useful feature in accepting our own aging. Sending and Receiving helps us keep a positive attitude and gives us something useful we can actually do when we are visiting the sick, tending to the dying, or reaching out to anyone we know, near or far, who needs our support.

Sending and Receiving is not a practice taught in my own Zen tradition. I learned it and now teach it in collaboration with a Western lama of the Tibetan Buddhist tradition. The version I describe here is an adaptation that conveys the essential spirit of the practice so that non-Buddhists and non-meditators can benefit from it. Although it may seem a bit elaborate, the practice, once learned, can in fact be done in as little as five or ten minutes.

PREPARATION

Sending and Receiving is best practiced in meditation posture, either in a chair or on a cushion. But once you have mastered it, you can practice it anywhere. Because the practice involves the imagination, most people find it easier to do it with eyes closed, although this is not necessary.

Practices of this type are often referred to as "visualization," but this is probably not the best word. "Imagination" is better. We all have a natural capacity to imagine, and we do it all the time. If I say, "Imagine the Statue of Liberty," you will immediately see it in your mind's eye. In fact, if you were hooked up to a brain scanner your visual cortex would light up in almost the same way as if you were actually looking at the real Statue of Liberty. In the same way, imagining generosity produces a feeling of real generosity.

The most important aspect of preparing for this practice is to recognize that everything we think and imagine emerges from and returns to what Buddhism calls "the great space of awareness." Before you imagine something, it was not there. After you finish imagining it, it is gone. Its reality is tentative: In the end, it is much like a dream. That said, dreams can be vitally important, and convey to us things we need to know.

Sending and Receiving is like this: a consciously guided waking dream for the benefit of another person as well as yourself. At the conclusion of the practice, you will return this dream to the same source of spacious awareness from which it came.

FINDING YOUR SPIRITUAL MENTOR

The next step in the preparation is to be conscious that you won't be producing generosity alone, which might be experienced by the ego as a burden and extra responsibility. Imagine instead that the generosity comes from your higher or awake self, which is true: Generosity is woven into the fabric of all existence. All living things give and receive all the time. The very act of breathing is a kind of giving and receiving. The circulation of energy is the real source of generosity. It's not something you need to kick-start, like a lawn mower engine.

Imagine that the ordinary you is being supported in this practice by a spiritual mentor, someone greater than yourself. It could be God or Buddha; it could be a spiritual person for whom you have great respect, like the Dalai Lama,

Gandhi, or Mother Teresa. Since I knew Shunryu Suzuki so well, and experienced his own generosity to me, I often think of him helping me send and receive.

Imagine the generous energy of this higher being resting in your heart. The generous feeling of your spiritual mentor is probably already resting in your heart. Let go of the notion that you have to be generous. Even though you may not feel particularly generous, you can borrow the generosity from your spiritual mentor to help you do this practice.

AWAKENING THE HEART CENTER

The "heart center" is the place where Sending and Receiving happens. The heart center is a little below the physical heart. It is the place where you feel the living sensations of giving and receiving. These sensations are normal and everyone has them; our language reflects that. We say "my heart went out to her," our sympathies are "heartfelt," we do things "wholeheartedly"; we are occasionally "heartbroken." These words and phrases refer to the sensations we feel in the heart center when the emotions of generosity—or its lack—touch us.

Touch your heart center with your hand to help awaken these sensations. Sending and Receiving invokes these sensations to create a flow of energy that you can actually feel. It is a good feeling.

Next, imagine a small sphere of brilliant white light in your heart center. This white light is a visual representation of the awakened mind. The white light need not be precise; think of it as a sense of energy or illumination in the center of your chest.

BREATHING INTO THE HEART CENTER

Sending and Receiving follows the path of the breath. So now feel the circulation of breathing in and breathing out flowing through the sphere of light in your heart center. On each in-breath, feel the breath coming in from the world and refreshing the sphere of light. On each out-breath, feel the breath going back out into the world with that light's generous energy.

Do this for a while until you can feel some sensation of flow or movement in your heart center. Even if all you feel is a subtle quality of awareness or energy, that is fine. Generosity is not a thought; it is a feeling. Remember the word "heartfelt." That is the feeling.

GENEROSITY TO YOURSELF

According to Buddhist thinking, it is difficult to be truly generous to another until you can first be generous to yourself. People in the helping professions such as doctors, nurses, therapists, and counselors sometimes forget this, and expend so much energy helping others that they forget to take care of themselves. Burnout is the result. To prevent it, this aspect of the practice asks you to try to picture an image of yourself, just as you are, sitting facing yourself from a few feet away, as though you were looking in a mirror. Some people actually use a mirror to get used to this idea.

It may seem at first like one too many things to imagine: first the spiritual mentor, then the sphere of white light, and now a mirror image of yourself! Don't worry; relax and let the various elements of the exercise find their way. It's not like juggling; you don't have to keep every element in view all the time. For now, concentrate on the mirror image of yourself sitting in front of you.

Once you've stabilized an image of yourself, begin to let your breath circulate generosity to and from the image of yourself. Breathing in, welcome all the difficulties and worries you may have into your heart center. The white light is a kind of furnace that incinerates those negative worries and impulses and turns them into generosity. As you breathe out, return that generosity back to yourself.

GENEROSITY TO YOURSELF AS AGING

As you do the practice, maintain a light, spontaneous attitude. Remember, the point of the practice is to be generous! Don't worry if the practice seems complicated or awkward at first. Everything in it is natural. It is natural to think of a spiritual mentor, or to feel loving sensations in your heart. It may seem a little less natural to picture a mirror image of yourself in front of you, but you undoubtedly do it every morning in front of the bathroom mirror!

Once you have become comfortable with receiving difficulty as you breathe in, and sending generosity as you breathe out, try changing the mirror image of yourself. Try imagining yourself five or ten years older. How will you look and feel? What worries and difficulties might you have then?

Fill in the details of this "older you" and continue the practice of Sending and Receiving. Concentrate particularly on sending the white light of generosity from your heart center to the "older you." Feel whatever feelings you might have about the "older you": regret, sadness, curiosity, excitement, confusion.

Now imagine the "older you" ten more years older. Continue the practice. How is it now? What has changed? Keep sending generosity; keep receiving whatever worries this older "older you" may have.

Go as far as you want to. Can you go as far as ninety? When I went to my financial adviser recently, I was taken aback to hear him casually refer to our financial situation at age ninety. With all my illnesses, I realized I never had pictured myself living that long. It may be that I won't. But I have tried practicing Sending and Receiving for myself at ninety. It was a strange feeling.

Try it.

You can be creative with this exercise and go backward in time too. Picture yourself as ten, fifteen, or twenty years younger, and send generous thoughts to that "younger you." A logician might say, "That 'younger you' no longer exists!" but in memory he or she certainly does. That "younger you" may need kindness and generosity every bit as much as some "older you."

GENEROSITY TO OTHERS

It should be clear by now that Sending and Receiving can be practiced with an image of anyone: your parents, your children, a friend who is ill, collective victims of a near or distant disaster. Although the practice is easiest for people you care about, it is possible to work up to doing this practice even for people you dislike. In fact, it can have great benefit when performed with such people in mind.

SENDING AND RECEIVING SLIDESHOW

I have often made it a practice to do Sending and Receiving as a kind of generosity "slideshow." I picture all the people I am thinking about, care about, or am concerned about one after another. I bring each of them to mind one at a time and practice Sending and Receiving for five or ten breaths. Then I go on to the next person. I don't necessarily sit in meditation posture. I do this sometimes when I first wake up. Another good time to do this exercise is just before you go to bed.

One of the inevitable consequences of growing older is that each of us has an ever-expanding list of people who need our prayerful thoughts. After I have imagined the individuals who need my attention, I often add groups of people near and far—victims of a recent disaster, for example. In this way I turn the sense of helplessness I sometimes feel when reading the day's headlines into something positive.

A skeptic might ask, "Will any of this *really* help? Is it really valuable and worth doing?" I answer as the Buddha did in response to the many questions his followers and critics frequently asked him: "Try it and see."

Don't believe it just because I say it, the Buddha would explain. Try it and see.

DISSOLVING THE IMAGE

As the final step in the practice of Sending and Receiving, it is important to dissolve all the creations of your imagination and let them dissipate into the vast space of awareness.

Begin with the objects of your generosity. Open your eyes, take a few deep breaths, and as you breathe out, imagine all the various people—including yourself—that you have imagined sitting before you slowly dissolve and vanish, like a slow fade on a movie screen. When their dissolution is complete, take one or two more "clear" breaths to make sure there is no residual imagination clinging to them.

Next, let the white light in your heart center fade away until it is nothing but empty space. In the same way, let the heart sensations and emotions that Sending and Receiving may have engendered flow out and disperse with each outbreath.

Finally, let any thoughts of your spiritual mentor fade away too. Let everything dissolve until there is nothing left but the ordinary sensations, the ordinary sights and sounds of you sitting in a room, relaxed and at rest.

This last step of letting everything dissolve is perhaps the most important of all. There is real power in bringing to mind all the people we care about and have strong feelings about, including ourselves. You created that power out of nothing, through your own imagination, and you can now release that power by letting it return to whence it came.

CHAPTER 10

Touching Divine Nature

Once at a conference for encephalitis survivors, I found myself at dinner seated next to a retired navy chaplain whom everyone called Colonel Bill. He was there because his adult son had, like me, come back to life after being given up for lost.

As we talked, it came out that he was a Baptist and I was a Buddhist. I thought he might find this off-putting, but it didn't seem to bother him. He seemed more interested in my story of recovery.

I told him about being unaware of the outside world but conscious inside my coma, realizing that I was at death's door and fighting to survive. "I fought and fought. Finally, I realized there was nothing I could do," I told him. "I surrendered. From that moment on I knew I was going to be all right. I felt that something was taking care of me."

Colonel Bill nodded. "I was waiting for you to say that."

He told me he had had a similar experience when he was young, riding across the country in a freezing boxcar with other G.I.s to a hospital in San Francisco. "I was burning up with scarlet fever. I knew I wasn't going to make it. I was too sick. That's when I surrendered to the higher power, and from then on it took care of me," he said. "I was called to become a chaplain that night."

Then he asked, "What do you Buddhists call that higher power? Do you call it God?"

I explained that Buddhists don't typically call it God, though throughout the world they pray to some form of Buddha as a higher power. Buddhism has terms like "the absolute," "genuine reality," "emptiness," and "awakened nature" to speak of a reality beyond individual personality or identity. There are many books that discuss these doctrines in detail, and I won't add to them here. I have already mentioned that in an interfaith context I sometimes use the term "divine nature," but I didn't that night with Colonel Bill. It didn't seem necessary. I just spoke of my experience of surrender.

In this chapter I share my deeply personal experiences as a person of Buddhist faith and explain some of the teachings and stories from the Buddhist tradition that support and underpin that faith. Buddhist readers will find this familiar. If you are not Buddhist, I hope that you can connect with my experience even if that is not the form or vehicle that your faith takes. There may also be some readers who find my account outside their comfort range. I ask those readers to approach what I say in a spirit of curiosity and inquiry. I can only speak of what is true for me and what I know.

What Happens When We Die?

The universal question for all of us who are beginning to face our own mortality is, "Where am I headed? What will happen when I die?" As a Zen priest, I am asked that question a lot, and Buddhism offers a richness of teachings on the subject. Let me begin by telling the story of Natasha, who came to see me during a meditation retreat. She was crying. Her best friend had just died after a long illness and she didn't know how to take care of her friend, or her grief. "Where has she gone?" Natasha said. "How can I help her? What happens when a person dies?"

I understood Natasha's conundrum. There is no deeper truth than sitting at someone's bedside, watching them take their last breath, and seeing the whole of their life—their entire personality and history—vanish suddenly.

I sat with Natasha for a while before responding to her question. I wanted to wait until all the layers of her question—her own grief, her desire to do something for her friend, and her questioning in the face of life's ultimate mystery—to settle before I said anything.

Finally I said, "They dissolve into light."

The next day, Natasha told me, she watched cumulus clouds drifting over distant mountains, and in their light she saw her friend. She said good-bye that way, in the light of the passing afternoon.

I did not offer Natasha a Buddhist teaching, or some abstract theory of dying, although I could have done so. Instead, I just offered her my own experience. Many years before, in the depths of my coma, I had had a detailed vision of a group of South American shamans gathered around my still body, gesturing and chanting in an ancient ceremony of healing. The oldest of these men explained to me that they were trying to turn me into a bird in order to liberate me and bring me back to life, but that in order to do this I would first have to die. I wanted more than anything to be healed and to come back. So I answered, "All right, I will die."

In the vision, I made my breath stop and waited for death to come. Suddenly I dissolved into a light that was both like the midnight sky and at the same time brilliantly white—infinitely spacious and enormously comforting. That was how I experienced death inside my coma vision.

I don't know for sure if this is what will actually happen when I truly die. But I do know that since that experience I'm not at all worried about dying. When I came out of the coma, I felt that now I knew how to die. My experience has made me comfortable with the thought of dying. Death no longer frightens me. When people tell me about their own fear of death and apprehension about it, I sometimes quote Stephen Levine, an early pioneer in the hospice movement who liked to say, with mordant humor, "Don't worry. Dying is perfectly safe." After my coma experience I have a sense of what he means. It did feel perfectly safe.

There is another way that we will know how to die when the time comes—not just because our body has resources that wake up and help us then—because we are actually dying all the time.

Living and Dying on Each Moment

In Buddhism, living and dying are not two different things. Instead, living and dying happen together—"on each moment," as Shunryu Suzuki liked to say. Every breath repeats this cycle. We breathe in and life comes. We breathe out and life goes. We say we "expire." Eventually a day will come when that out-breath will truly be our last. Until then, we live and die on each moment. I used to wonder why Suzuki would say "*on* each moment" rather than "*in* each moment." I think it was because for him "on" more accurately described the physicality of his experience, the actual feeling of exhaling. As he said, "Exhaling, you gradually fade into empty, white paper. Inhaling without effort you naturally come back to yourself." He also said, "When you do this practice, you cannot easily become angry . . . the great joy for us is exhaling rather than inhaling."[18]

So for a Buddhist, dying is not some unusual thing to wonder about or be frightened of. Dying is something that is part of our ordinary activity. All around us, things change and pass away. But thinking of our own eventual passing, we still ask, "What happens? Where will I go?"

Where Did They Go?

A classical Zen story turns on the question, "Where did they go?"

Baso, the teacher, and Hyakujo, the disciple, were walking on a country road. Suddenly a flock of wild geese flew by.

Baso pointed up and said, "What are those?"

Hyakujo replied, "They are wild geese."

Baso said, "Where have they gone?"

Hyakujo said, "They have flown away."

Suddenly Baso reached out and twisted Hyakujo's nose, shouting, "Yet they have been here from the very first!"

It is said that Hyakujo achieved a spiritual breakthrough at that moment.

Like many Zen teaching stories, this anecdote—well-known to students of Zen—is rather cryptic and requires some explanation. Baso begins with a curiously ordinary question, "What are those?" Hyakujo's response is also conventional. Given Baso and Hyakujo's long and intimate relationship, we suspect that something unconventional might be percolating under the surface of these naïve statements. Baso and Hyakujo were Zen monks. Spiritual inquiry was their lifelong business, so this exchange is about more than geese. Baso is saying, in effect, "Here's something that seems ordinary, geese in flight. How do you see it?" And Hyakujo's reply is, in effect, "I see it conventionally."

Baso's next probe also seems conventional. He asks, "Where have they gone?" But there is now an edge to his question. He's saying, "I'm not interested in where they seem to have gone—that's obvious—but what their coming and going means in spiritual terms."

Hyakujo missed Baso's spiritual edge. He stayed in the ordinary. He just repeated the obvious: They have flown away.

Baso suddenly reached out and twisted Hyakujo's nose. He wanted Hyakujo to pay closer attention: No! Don't stick to the conventional. This moment is a window into the great mystery, the mystery of life and death. You have been a Zen monk for many years. This mystery is your business. What do you have to say about it right now?

Suddenly Hyakujo understood. His teacher's question was about being here and then being gone, about life and death itself. From the conventional point of view we are born, we live, we die, and then we vanish—just like the geese. But from a spiritual perspective that is not the whole story. There is more to living and dying than just being here and then being gone. Some essential part of us—the part I call "divine nature"—was here before we were born and will be here after we die. It is not our personality or our individuality; the person known as Lew Richmond was not here before 1947 and someday will completely disappear. But the aspect of Lew Richmond that is like brilliant awareness doesn't come or go any more than the clear blue sky in which the geese flew doesn't come or go. That aspect exists in an eternal present. This is not just a Buddhist doctrine. William Blake, a poet and preeminent European mystic, described it as "eternity in an hour." Baso was pointing out to Hyakujo the eternity in each flying goose.

Living and Dying

Once, in the sixties, during the cold war, a student of Suzuki Roshi asked him, "If every human being on planet Earth vanishes, what will happen to Buddhism?"

"It will continue," Suzuki calmly replied.

His comment used to seem mysterious to me, but now it doesn't. Deep inside my coma, when I experienced myself dissolving into light, I felt that I would continue, not as Lew Richmond the individual, but as the light. The light felt cozy and familiar, like my childhood home. I still feel that light all around me today. I believe it is the same light that illuminates everyone. When I exhale, my breath dissolves into the light, and when I inhale, my breath comes in out of that light. It is an ordinary thing.

This is my faith as a Buddhist. I think the reason that Colonel Bill and I got along is that we spoke that same language of the spirit. It wasn't necessary to have a discussion about Buddhists versus Baptists.

It came out that he had had the same experience at his son's bedside that my wife, Amy, had had at mine. The doctors had come to him and told him to prepare himself; the news wasn't good.

"Did you believe them?" I said to Colonel Bill.

"No," he said.

"What did you do?"

"I held my son's hand and prayed."

As the encephalitis survivors' conference finished up, everyone checked out and went to get their cars. Colonel

Bill's son was one of the last to leave. Like me, he had recovered completely and was full of energy. In fact, he was the one who had organized the conference.

"Good-bye," I said, shaking his hand.

"Good-bye, brother," he said with a wink.

I hope Colonel Bill and his son, wherever they are, are well. I consider them fellow travelers on the journey of aging, and my good teachers in the mystery of living and dying.

The Candle Flame

Buddhism does speak of a reality beyond individual personality or identity, and I experienced that when I dissolved into light. But it was not as though the light existed on its own and I joined it. The light and I were never two separate things.

There are two ways to describe ourselves. According to one way we will grow old and die, and according to another we have always been here, just like Hyakujo's geese. Buddhism speaks of "form and emptiness" or "relative and absolute" to explain this, but I prefer to use the image of a candle flame.

One way to look at the candle flame is to see it as always new, ever-changing. Every moment the flame is different, just as in every moment each breath we take is new. The wind blows the flame, mist dampens it, conditions change it, just as in our long life many things occur. Our personal history is unique. When we are born, the candle is tall, and as we age the candle grows shorter and shorter. One day it will be gone.

Another way of looking at the candle flame is to see it as light. Regardless of whether the flame is strong or weak, or whether the candle is tall or short, the light is the same. It burns as brightly whether the candle is tall, medium, or short—whether we are at the beginning of our life, in the middle, or near the end. One day our individual light may go out, but light itself continues because light is everywhere: in the sky, in the sun, in the stars, in the whole universe. The individual candle flame burns down and goes out. It dies. But the light of the universe, of which that flame is one particular instance, does not.

Whether we live or whether we die, the candle flame burns just the same. That light is who we most deeply are, and we can rest in that light at any time simply by relaxing into it and surrendering to it.

Contemplative Reflection: Resting in Awareness

THE SPACE OF AWARENESS

I have said earlier that there are two aspects to meditation: focus and insight. Both require effort. But there is also a kind of contemplation that is beyond effort. In fact the effort needed to practice it is to let go of what we usually think of as effort and completely relax.

In Zen we call this "just sitting" or "just awareness." In the Tibetan Buddhist tradition it is called "resting in true nature" or "natural great perfection." Whatever it is called, it is the highest meditation because it is not meditation *on* something, but rather a resting in our true nature. It is just a state of being completely present, just as we are.

I have spoken of my own experience of dissolving into light, and this practice of "just awareness" is like that, except that "dissolving" implies that something happens. It implies that first we are here, and then we dissolve. Actually, there is no dissolving. We are already awareness itself. It is just a matter of resting in it.

This practice is best done in meditation posture, either in a chair or on a cushion. Traditionally the eyes are somewhat open. To keep the eyes open means that we don't go anywhere or enter some other state. We are already where we need to be. Our ordinary perception of sights, sounds, and smells is good just as it is.

It is helpful to ground your awareness in the breath just long enough for your attention to fill your body. Feel your body in space; feel the space around your body. Feel that space *is* your body. The feeling is as though your breath is like a liquid, and that liquid pours into every corner of your body and fills it up. In the Tibetan tradition, there is an instruction to "mingle space and awareness." This is an advanced instruction, but its meaning is simple. Our awareness is like space in that it has no form or shape. It doesn't have a limit or boundary, either. If you ask awareness to fill the room in which you are sitting, instantly you feel it. Your awareness becomes as large as the room. If you ask your awareness to become even bigger, to include the whole house or building where you are, it does that.

But awareness is not exactly the same as space. Space is something scientific, like outer space or a vacuum. Space isn't a *thing*. Space is the container for other things. Awareness is different. Awareness is alive, and it is conscious and awake.

When I was in a coma, I had no sense of having a body or of being in a hospital room. All my ordinary senses were shut down. But I was aware and awake. I was alive, and when the doctors did an electrical scan of my brain, it looked normal.

So where was my awareness, where was my consciousness? To the doctors, or to my wife, I was immobile and inert. But to myself, I existed in the space of awareness. For me, space and awareness were mingled, and in that world I dreamed and had visions.

In the Tibetan tradition, this mind state is called *bardo*, and it means "the in-between." One of the *bardos* is the world between life and death. After my recovery, I asked teachers of that tradition if I had been in the *bardo*, and when I described it they said yes.

The *bardo* can also mean our ordinary life, the one that unfolds between the moment of birth and the moment of death. It is the space of awareness wherever you are. Rest in that alive space. Don't try to do anything with it. Surrender to it; relax in it; enjoy it.

Thoughts will come. Distractions will arise. Let them be.

They are just passing visitors in the space of awareness, like small, harmless insects or patterns of light on the wall. The space of awareness includes them. In fact, it includes everything. In the space of awareness, there is no outside. There is no "I am here" and "the world is there." Everything is a welcome guest in the vast space of awareness.

BASIC GOODNESS

The moment-by-moment effort of Resting in Awareness is letting go of each thing as soon as it arises. If an unpleasant thought arises, let it go. If a pleasant thought arises, do the same. If thoughts of the past come, remember that they are just welcome guests in the garden party of awareness. If thoughts of the future come, let them pass through on their way to the garden.

There is nothing to do, nothing to achieve. Allow yourself to feel completely taken care of, as I did when I felt myself dissolve into light, or as Colonel Bill did when he surrendered to the higher power in the freezing boxcar. There is no need to improve, no need to be different than you already are. How you are in this moment is enough.

When I said to the Christian talk show host that we Buddhists pray in silence to touch our divine nature, this is what I meant. I know some Buddhists have a problem with the word "divine." It sounds to them too much like God. But "divine" can also just mean "wonderful."

In the same way, Resting in Awareness touches our divine nature because the feeling is good. Trungpa Rinpoche, an early pioneer in bringing Tibetan Buddhism to the West, liked to translate the term "Buddha nature" as "basic goodness." I really like that phrase. If we did nothing more in our spiritual life than relate to people by noticing their basic goodness, that would be a lot. Resting in Awareness means resting in our own basic goodness.

BASIC GOODNESS AND AGING

This practice is not something to do only because it feels good. Resting in Awareness can be the deepest spiritual practice of aging. Remember the candle: Regardless of whether the candle itself is long, medium, or short, the flame of awareness burns just as brightly. Regardless of whether we are forty, sixty, eighty, or older, Resting in Awareness and touching our divine nature is a way to be ageless.

"They have been there from the very first!" Baso was not just talking about geese; he was talking about you. You have been here from the very first. You are here now, Resting in Awareness, and as you age and grow more infirm, you will still be here.

A contemporary Tibetan meditation teacher once gave a lecture about "just being here" and a student asked him, "What about if someone gets Alzheimer's? Will they still be here?"

The teacher replied, "Their mental faculties are damaged, and their personality erodes, but their essence is unchanged."

And when the day comes that you are ready to die, you will still just be here too. I asked a good friend, an eminent Western teacher of Tibetan Buddhism, what his tradition taught about how to prepare for dying. I knew that in his tradition, there were many techniques and rituals that could be done. I wanted to know what he thought.

He said, "All my teachers taught that when that moment comes, just rest in awareness. Do nothing more than that."

In other words, by practicing "just awareness" today, and tomorrow, and regularly as your life proceeds, you will have done everything you need to do to prepare for that final moment.

That final moment will actually be no different from this or any other moment. Although your friends and family will see you disappear, you will not actually dissolve into light. You are already light, right now. You will dissolve into light the way water dissolves into water. You disappear into something that you already are.

When asked directly what will happen when we die, Shunryu Suzuki said, "Don't worry. Nothing is going to happen."

I watched him slowly die. I was young and distraught and had never seen anyone slowly die. What was extraordinary is that he was just the same as he had always been. He laughed, he joked, he wandered around our Zen center greeting people who came and talked quietly to each of us he met.

I kept thinking, "When will he change? When will he acknowledge this terrible thing that is about to happen?"

He never did. When that final morning came, he summoned his chief disciple. When the chief disciple came into Suzuki's bedroom, Suzuki took one last look, breathed out a final long breath, and didn't breathe in again.

That was all. Nothing special happened, because for his whole life that was how Suzuki lived. Each time he breathed out, he was ready for it to be his last. So he had no fear and appreciated each new breath when it came.

That was his greatest teaching to me and to all who knew him. I have tried my whole life to follow his way. I hope when that time comes for me, I can rest in awareness as simply and quietly as he did.

CHAPTER 11

What Doctors Know

Everywhere you look, aging research is in the news. Every week, it seems, some new finding is reported. Some of these are helpful, and some can be confusing. Often, results of studies seem to contradict each other. Recently a team of researchers led by psychologist Charles Holahan of the University of Texas, Austin, concluded that moderate drinkers live longer, on average, than nondrinkers. What was really surprising was the finding that even *heavy* drinkers live longer than nondrinkers in spite of their alcohol-related health issues.[19] As individuals trying to age well and live healthy lives, what are we to make of such reports? Scientists themselves aren't sure. There was controversy about whether to even publicize the results out of concern that they could contradict decades of medical advice about the dangers of drinking.

Scientific studies of this sort look at large groups of people, trying to discern patterns and statistical significances. But doctors see patients one at a time. For them each patient is unique. What can these physicians tell us about aging well?

To help me learn more, I interviewed several doctors, among them primary care physicians, a specialist in rehabilitation medicine, a physical therapist, psychiatrists, and psychologists. These physicians aren't researchers, but clinicians. Their patients are people they've known intimately for many years, if not decades. Each of these doctors taught me something valuable about the aging process; all of them together taught me that when it comes to aging, everyone is different.

Men and Women

One issue that interested me was the difference in how the genders experience aging. In my interviews with both men and women, I recognized some differences but didn't know whether they were due to gender or were just individual variations. For example, Stephanie and Christina both seemed to have made a good adjustment to growing older and could speak lightheartedly about it. In contrast, Alan and Greg were both having a hard time adjusting to the changes of aging. Do women adjust more easily to aging than men?

When I posed this question to the doctors, they immediately honed in on one clear difference: Women face aging sooner and more realistically because they go through menopause. "When it comes to realizing they're aging," one said, "women drop off a cliff, so to speak, while men the same age either ignore the signs or notice them a lot more gradually."

While menopausal women have a whole range of symptoms that are quite noticeable and measurable—hot flashes, loss of bone density (more than in men), diminished endurance, disturbed sleep, and mood changes—men in their fifties who are active and in good health still feel very much as they did in their thirties and forties. If they are athletic—as Alan was—they try to compete and stay in shape. When they overdo it, "weekend warrior" sports injuries occur. One M.D. told me about a fifty-two-year-old male patient of his who broke his ankle boogie-boarding at the beach with his son. At the hospital, the man told him, "You know, Doc, I finally get it. I'm not eighteen anymore." Another male patient of middle age fell off his bike, smashed his helmet, and sustained a mild concussion. He was lucky; that injury could have killed him.

A third justified his penchant for running in races with men half his age by saying, "I'm an old Marine. If aging is going to get me, I'm not going to go quietly."

Data and Humor

Another gender difference is that women tend to use humor more in dealing with aging, while men—once they get past their denial—prefer serious data and hard facts. A woman doctor specializing in menopause told me that some of her patients keep a whole second closet of clothes that no longer fit them. Women who have put on weight say, "Why don't I give all those clothes away to the cancer consignment store?" Then they answer themselves, "Well, one of these days I'll really get serious about going to the gym, and I'll be able to wear all those clothes again."

Then they laugh.

When confronted by issues such as high blood pressure or cholesterol, more men than women may resort to what one doctor called the "denial saga." "My blood pressure is fine," the patient will say. "I had a big meal last night. That's all." Or he'll say, "Oh, I drank three cups of coffee this morning just before I came into your office. This isn't my real blood pressure."

One patient—a highly successful man in his early sixties—came into his doctor's office with blood pressure of 240 over 140. This is a malignant hypertension from which one can keel over and die at any time. "I tried to explain this to him," his doctor told me, "but he shrugged it off and said he felt fine."

So the doctor took a different tack. He asked the patient if he'd ever worked on car radiators. "Sure," the patient said. "I'm rebuilding an old MG in my garage as we speak." Then the doctor asked him if he'd ever seen a radiator hose burst. When the patient nodded, the doctor told him, "You've got radiator hoses all over your brain, and they're all about to burst.

"And that did it," his doctor said. "His denial dissolved before my eyes. I have a whole bag of tricks like that."

Once a male patient "gets it," he is likely to take the issue up as a problem to be solved, a challenge to be surmounted. "Male patients like to create charts and graphs, showing how they're improving," another doctor told me. "Or they'll have a program on their smartphone that tracks calorie intake. They prove to me they're winning. That's fine. I *want* them to win."

I also heard from the physicians I spoke with that women in their fifties and sixties often form support groups around their emerging interests—a book group, a gardening group, a hiking or bird-watching group—that can also serve as a forum in which to discuss age-related issues and problems, physical and otherwise. Men do this too—it is a good strategy for both genders—but their groups tend to be oriented more around sports, recreation, or hobbies. Men also seem to maintain their primary focus on career longer than women. Even highly successful career women enrich their lives by branching out into community service, volunteering, and local politics.

All the primary care physicians I spoke to tended to agree on these general patterns of gender differences, but they all made sure to stress that these differences are generalizations and that there is a lot of overlap in individual coping patterns and behaviors. The psychiatrists had a somewhat different take on gender differences in aging. Compared with the primary care physicians, who see all their patients regularly regardless of whether they are having problems, psychiatrists' patients are skewed toward those who are having difficulty. A psychologist who used projective testing such as the Rorschach to diagnose and hone in on patient problems reported that without names and faces, it is hard to discern gender from test results alone.

"You'd think with all the psychological factors these tests measure, if men and women were so different the tests would spot it," the psychologist said. "But in my experience that's not true. I've come to believe that if you put aside stereotypes and cultural assumptions, when it comes to midlife problems, men and women are more similar than they are different."

Loss and Identity

One category of aging that seems to affect both genders similarly involves loss and identity. We have seen throughout this book how many of aging's losses are irrevocable and cannot easily be mended. In talking about such losses, people often begin by saying, "There's no time left to . . ." or "I don't have so much time left . . ." or "I've got to make the most of the time I have." There is a poignancy and sadness to these expressions. If people's nest eggs lost value during the crash of 2008, they may well be too old to go back into the job market and earn it back. If a close friend or relative has died, they are gone forever.

When I talked to my psychiatrist friends about losses of aging, they agreed that as we age, the loss that is often the most difficult to deal with is loss of identity. We're always losing pieces of our identity. When we leave home and go off to college, that's a loss of our identity as a child. When we graduate from college and leave our dorm mates behind, that's a loss too. But when we're young, we don't have to work so hard to make up for those pieces of our identity that fall away. The world is always bringing new pieces to us.

No sooner do we graduate from college than we land our first job (or it used to be so before 10 percent unemployment!), with a major new identity that can make up for the sadness of leaving college life behind. When we get married, we leave behind the freedoms of single life, but we embark on an exciting new identity as a married person. When we have children, our identity becomes, in addition to our other roles, that of parent. Regarding our identity, throughout the first half of our life, loss and gain work in tandem without our noticing it much. When we are young, we expect the world to bring us new opportunities and fresh chances, and it often does; it's part of the magic of youth.

What's hard about the losses sustained in older age is that it's not so easy to repair the holes they leave in our identity. When we get to "the other side of the hill," as one psychiatrist termed it, the world doesn't bring us the new pieces; we have to find them ourselves. After a divorce, a new marriage doesn't automatically materialize. When we lose a job, a new job doesn't suddenly appear at our doorstep. When we are younger, the process of identity repair runs more or less under its own steam. When we're older, the job of identity repair is more and more up to us.

As we discussed in the chapter on elderhood, this state of affairs may be an artifact of modern life. In traditional societies, such as Native American cultures and others that still exist throughout the world, they provided elders with new roles and identities as their old ones fell away. As elders left behind their productive roles as providers and the responsibilities of parenthood, their community encouraged them to become storytellers and singers, healers, midwives, hospice workers; they became mentors to the younger adults who were themselves just taking on leadership roles. These are not jobs that the elders had to make up or concoct themselves; they were part of life.

How different for today's elderly in our world! As we approach retirement, we're pretty much on our own.

Dr. Houston was an air force psychiatrist in the 1970s when the military was just beginning to realize what problems retirement posed for career servicemen and -women. Retirees went from a highly structured life to one with hardly any structure at all, and the subsequent problems could be severe: depression, anxiety, substance abuse, even suicide. As a result, the military developed a multiyear program of retirement preparation.

I asked Dr. Houston how he helps his own aging patients facing retirement. He replied:

> If they're already retired, I have them walk me through a week. What do they do on Monday, Tuesday, Wednesday, and so on? I ask them, Where did you go, what did you do, who did you talk to? That gives me a jumping-off point to start talking about what's good about that and what's missing. Are they truly enjoying their activities? Is there something they've always wanted to do, like take a trip or

take up a hobby, that they imagine they're now too old to do? If you won the lottery, I ask, what would you do then? I get people to think outside the box, to draw in all the resources and excitement of their hopes and dreams, and out of that build a richer identity, one that finds replacements for the losses in their life.

Dr. Houston had concluded that although older people have to do the "heavy lifting" of a postretirement life themselves, they *can* do it. He sees it time and again. He was optimistic and told me that for many people, the postretirement years can be the best years of their life.

Good Worry and Bad Worry

Aging can be a time of increasing worry. For one thing, as we age we have more issues and people to worry about: friends, family, children, and a lifetime of important relationships, as well as obvious and perennial concerns about health, money, and security. The simple drumbeat of maintenance and paperwork—insurance forms and claims, home and auto repairs, financial reports, correspondence, e-mails, and endless filing—seems to steadily accelerate with each passing year. The longer we live, the more details there are to take care of.

And yet worry need not be an affliction. There is a side of what we call worry that is positive and can lead to solutions and insights. Dr. Eldridge talked to me about "healthy worries," concerns that are wholesome and necessary for us to attend to. The first one, he said, is simply, Are my needs being met, and if not, why not? The second, and equally important healthy worry, is, Who's in control of my destiny—me or someone or something else?

These, he went on to say, are worries you should pay attention to and do something about. If our needs are not being met, we eventually become angry, depressed, or both. If we don't pay attention to these basics, that is not so good. If we dwell too much on them and start to obsess about them, that's not good either. I said to him, "It sounds as though you are talking about a middle way."

He nodded. "Yep," he said. "That's right. There has to be a middle way."

The "middle way" is a core Buddhist teaching that has many nuances of meaning, one of which is a sense of balance or moderation. The Buddha taught that any spiritual practice is like a lute string. If it is too tight or too loose it does not make a good sound. Only when it is tuned just right can its music be heard.

Dr. Eldridge went on to explain that many people he sees are convinced that their worries defy solution simply because they don't have enough time left to fix them. If their nest egg lost value in the crash, they're too old now to earn it back. If their house has gone down in value, they expect they'll be dead before it regains its value.

If people become so depressed or discouraged in the face of such difficulties that they give up, that is having the lute string too slack. If they become angry, anxious, or frantic—if their lute string is too tight—that is not productive either. For people who are discouraged, Dr. Eldridge encourages them to do *something,* however small. "If people are struggling with financial reverses, I ask them to look for a way to save ten dollars a month," he said.

And for people who are obsessing on their problem to the exclusion of all else, Dr. Eldridge sends them on a trip— even if it is only a drive to the seashore and back.

In listening to Dr. Eldridge, I was reminded of one of my Buddhist teachers who liked to say, "Every breath, new chances." The not-so-obvious corollary to this teaching is, "At all costs, keep breathing."

Other psychiatrists echoed Dr. Eldridge's advice. We should spend enough time worrying to identify a problem, but not so long that we begin to dwell on it. It's preferable to move to solutions as quickly as possible. "If you worry too much for too long, your unconscious will become anxious and believe there is an immediate and impending danger," Dr. Eldridge summed up.

Use your worry like a radar to hone in on the target, but then attack your target with a bunch of possible solutions. For example, suppose you have a bad hip. You might start dwelling on that, and pretty soon you're thinking, "I'm not going to be able to walk, I'm not going to get around, I'll be in one of those mobile carts, I'll lose my strength, I won't be able to go out." You spin these problems into crises, and before you know it you're anxious, you're depressed, and you may be consulting a psychiatrist with a serious problem.

But all of that worry is just speculation. None of it may be true. Identify the problem and immediately figure out how you are going to get help, how you are going to deal with it. That's healthy worry.

Building a Team

All the psychiatrists and psychologists I spoke to mentioned that one important requirement as we get older is to build a team of helpers for the different problems we encounter. When we are young we have energy and stamina with which to attack our problems alone. As older men and women, we need a team: a good doctor, a good accountant, a good financial adviser, a good plumber, electrician, car mechanic, and so on. People who have the knack of team building often enjoy creating their team; it may be harder for others, but it's a necessity.

Just like the owner of a small business does, seek out possible team members, assess their skills and suitability, bring them in as part of your team, watch their performance, and do not trust them blindly. After Alan heard that his college friend had died suddenly, he realized—really for the first time in his life—that he needed help. He began asking around for a good therapist and began seeing one, but soon felt that it was not a good choice for him. He eventually settled on a sports psychologist. He dealt with his high blood pressure by beginning to study stress-reduction meditation and also began seeing an acupuncturist. As a track coach, Alan instinctively understood the process of team building, but it was a revelation to him that he needed to—and could successfully—build a team to help him with his life-stage needs.

Curiosity and Openness

The first questions I tended to ask my psychologist and psychiatrist interviewees were, "How does healthy aging look to you? What are the qualities you see?"

One quality they all spoke of was curiosity. People who are doing well with their aging have a deep interest in what is going on around them. If they're going on a trip, they do research on the Web to learn all about their destination. If there's a town meeting coming up to decide about the sewer system, they want to go and find out how it turns out. They've heard about a new restaurant from a friend and they can't wait to try it. And when they talk about these things, there's enthusiasm and energy in their voice. They're engaged in their life.

People who aren't doing so well with their aging tend to be the opposite. They tend to contract into a smaller world, one that is individual and personal. If they have illnesses or injuries, they dwell on them. If they have a problem, they worry it to death and can't seem to talk about anything else. For them, it's too much trouble to travel or to try out the new restaurant. They'd rather stay at home and watch TV or surf the Internet.

The Extraordinary Elderly

In the course of my interviews, I kept hearing the term "the extraordinary elderly." These are people who seem to have beaten the odds when it comes to aging. Though they might be in their eighties or even nineties, their state of mind seems eternally young.

Earlier we met two people—Emma and Sarah—whom we might place among the extraordinary elderly. Emma, the artist with arthritis who overcame difficult health obstacles to find a different way to paint, was extraordinary in the sense that she refused to let the physical obstacles of old age defeat her. Sarah, though rather frail physically at age 105, was full of energy, with a mischievous sparkle in her eye. She seemed to love everything she saw or touched, from her ethereal weavings to the texture of the couscous and tomato salad she ate slowly, forkful by forkful, as she talked to me.

The extraordinary elderly are everywhere. Most of us know one or two—perhaps even a parent or relative—who have refused to "go gentle into that good night," as Dylan Thomas wrote. How do they do it? I told Dr. Houston about Emma and Sarah and asked him to comment. Did he know what secret sauce such people were drinking?

"Yes," he said, "I see these people from time to time. They all have that incredible curiosity and enthusiasm for what is going on around them. They'll tell me they're in the middle of a wonderful book and have to run home to find out how it ends. Even if you talk to them about dying, they're not afraid. If anything, they're annoyed that dying might interrupt all the fascinating things they're doing."

At the end of Nikos Kazantzakis' novel *Zorba the Greek*, a villager describes the last words of Zorba, a man whose enthusiasm and zest for life was unparalleled.

"I've done heaps and heaps of things in my life, but I still did not do enough. Men like me should live a thousand years . . ." These were his last words. He then sat up in bed, threw back the sheets and tried to get up. We ran to prevent him . . . but he brushed us all roughly aside, jumped out of bed and went to the window. There, he gripped the frame, looked out far into the mountains, opened wide his eyes and began to laugh, then to whinny like a horse. It was thus, standing, with his nails dug into the window frame, that death came to him.[20]

The fictional Zorba could be the exemplar of all extraordinary elders. He represents those people in every country and society who defy the odds and expectations of aging's decline with the power of their zest for life.

Contemplative Reflections

THE OLD AND THE NEW

This contemplative exercise focuses on identity—the way we lose old pieces of our identity as we age, and the opportunity to create new identities to replace what we have lost.

This can be a pencil-and-paper exercise or a mental reflection while seated quietly in a calm, supportive environment.

Begin by asking yourself the question, In the last three, five, or ten years, what pieces of my identity have I lost? Has it been something physical: an injury, a chronic condition, an incipient illness such as high blood pressure, diabetes, or heart arrhythmia?

Is it connected to my work identity? Have I lost a job, been passed over for a promotion, recently retired, or changed professions in a way that leaves me less satisfied?

Has it had to do with financial identity? Did I lose a lot of money in the 2008 crash? Did my home go down in value? Have I had to cut into my nest egg to help a struggling adult child or other relative?

Has it been something personal? Have I recently lost a friend to death or illness? Has a longtime relationship recently ended? Have old friends drifted away or moved away?

Take an inventory of your losses of identity and tune in to the feelings that come with loss: loneliness, sadness, grief, wistfulness, even anger.

Now shift to the positive side of the ledger and ask yourself, During that same time period, what new aspects of my identity have come in to replace what I have lost? Have I taken up a new hobby or vocation? Have I launched a new business or found a new way to supplement my income? Have I started a new relationship? What have you already done to fill in the gaps and crevices that the losses of aging have brought you?

Now, as a third step, imagine new possibilities to replenish your identity that you have not yet tried or put into practice. Reach as high and as far as you can.

A Day Away

CHAPTER 12

A Day Away—
Preparation

Aging is a time to get to know yourself in new ways—to open yourself to gifts unavailable to youth—by forging a deeper connection to your inner life. Thus far this book has offered many approaches and methods for doing that. As our journey continues, I would like to offer one more: the "day away." Spending a day by yourself in spiritual retreat is an excellent way to deepen and consolidate all that we have discussed and all that you have learned. This day can be a gift to others as well as yourself, and may radiate benefit far and wide. The next three chapters will guide you step by step through the process of planning and performing your day away.

At first blush a day by yourself may seem isolating. But it is not so. The spiritual life is all about connection—connection to oneself as well as to others. Both are necessary, and their balance changes as we age. The first half of life, the uphill slope, is a time when we forge a lifetime of external connections—with job, career, partner or spouse, children, friends, professional relationships, church or spiritual center. That outer work of connecting becomes a defining part of who we are in terms of outer personality. The second half of life—the so-called downhill slope—is a time when these outer connections can be joined and strengthened by inner ones, as we reflect on the meaning of all that we have done and the kind of person we have become and still want to be.

Your day away will not be overly strenuous or long—it will last from 9 A.M. to 5 P.M. (or less if you choose to do only half a day). "Nine to five" used to signify a day of work—a time span that seems quaint today, as more and more people work long hours of unpaid overtime and are hostage to the e-mail-driven seven-day workweek. Nevertheless, the phrase "nine to five" still connotes a workday, and your day away is simply a different kind of work, separated from usual routines. Buddhist readers who have experienced meditation retreats will be comfortable with this concept. But other readers have their own familiar versions: a visit to an all-day spa, a fishing weekend, a long hike alone by the seashore. Most of us already have hand-crafted versions of a time apart from the routines of ordinary life.

Daily routines are like waves on the surface of the ocean. If that's all we know, we're missing all that the ocean is. Periodically we should dive below. Only then can we fully

experience the calm substance of deeper water, and understand that the surface waves are just a part of the ocean's
nature, not the whole.

Yet today, more than ever, we skim the surface of the
ocean waves. Cell phones and smartphones, texting, Skyp-
ing, and e-mails keep us focused on moment-to-moment
ephemeral things. I myself have not been immune. My Android phone goes with me everywhere and informs me
with a variety of clicks and tones when I have an e-mail, an
appointment, or a task to do. Many Buddhist teachers I
know are similarly wired in. Even the young Tibetan lamas
are electronically connected, and e-mail and text with the
rest of us. That is in contrast to the years I spent in a monastery in the 1970s, where there were no phones, no electricity, and no heat, and most of the technical marvels that
seem indispensable to us now had not yet been invented.
And yet I felt more deeply connected to others and to my
own inner life at that time than at any other. What kind of
world have we fashioned that makes us feel connected only
when we are electronically amplified? We all need a holiday
from time to time. In medieval Europe there were forty or
fifty saint days a year. On those days routines were set
aside; religious observance and feasting were the norm.
Easter and Christmas are vestiges of this once rich calendar. Those researching today's teenagers are concerned
that today's constantly texting youth may have real difficulty forging deep human connections as adults.

In such a world, a day away can be like a healing lotion—
a way to reconnect with universal basics. This daylong

retreat can be a time to reflect on the life you have lived—
and the life you would like to live.

Preparation

The first step in preparing for your day away is to reflect on
what you hope to gain from it. Because this personal retreat
is just for you, it will happen in your own zone of privacy.
No one will know what you do; no one will be keeping
score. The only arbiter of success is yourself, and the only
standard of comparison will be your own aspirations for it.
A note for readers who have attended group meditation retreats: The personal retreat is different and in some ways
requires more initiative and effort. In a group retreat you
turn yourself over to the planners of the retreat and just
follow along. There your most important job is to show up.

In planning for the personal retreat, you need to establish your motivations in advance, make all the appropriate
preparations, and promise yourself that you will not post-
pone or reschedule unless there is a very important reason
to do so. This retreat is not like a date you can cancel if
something more pleasant comes up. It is a date to spend a
day or half day with your closest and dearest friend—
yourself! It is never selfish or self-absorbed to do a personal
retreat in the service of inner and outer connection.

As a way of firming up your intention and keeping it vibrant in the days and weeks leading up to your scheduled
day away, I recommend leaving yourself "spiritual Post-its"
a few weeks before the date and putting them where you

have to see them—stuck to your computer, next to the bed, or on your bathroom mirror. I relied on spiritual Post-its when I was recovering from my brain illness. Every time I got discouraged during my long healing, I created slogans to encourage myself, and posted them where I couldn't miss them. One of them read, "I'm better than I was last week, and next week I'll be better than I am now." Another was a kind of poem that came to me in a vision:

> This is a journey.
> The journey is a river.
> The river is long.
> Follow the river.

At the time those Post-its really carried me along.

Here's another good one. Write this out on a card, a Post-it, or a piece of paper, and read it back to yourself: "This personal retreat is for everyone as well as for me." How can it be both? It is both because outer and inner connections are two halves of the same intimacy. To know ourselves on the inside opens us up to knowing others on the outside.

Another recommended Post-it goes like this:

When I return from my day away I will be _____
_____ and I will
do the following: _____
_____.

On my own recent personal retreat, I filled in these blanks this way: "When I return I will be more patient, and I will make a list of my friends who are ill and call them." Such messages left in prominent places will allow the purpose of your upcoming day away to gestate and grow.

Once you have set a date for your day away, internally your retreat has already begun. Your mind will be at work imagining it, and your Post-it intentions will be germinating.

Reading

During your day away you will be practicing many of the contemplative reflections already described in the book— Aging Breath by Breath in Chapter 2; Gratitude Walk in Chapter 4; Vertical Time in Chapter 5; the Loving Kindness Prayer in Chapter 7; Calm Lake in Chapter 8; and Resting in Awareness in Chapter 10. Although the method, style, and context of these practices will be somewhat different during your day away than the way they were described in their chapters, it will help you to read through their descriptions and refamiliarize yourself with them. This is something you can do in the days before your retreat.

The Place

Give thought to where your retreat will take place, whether in some undisturbed part of your own house, or in a room at a hotel or resort. Weather permitting, you might spend your day away outdoors—or put together some combination of venues.

When you've decided the home/landscape of your retreat, use the following checklist:

Prepare your place for your comfort with a comfortable chair and pillows, and warm enough clothing.

Prepare food and drink to have during the course of the retreat. Mindful food preparation can be part of your day away.

Walking is part of the day's practice. Decide ahead of time where you will walk, perhaps have a backpack available, and water, comfortable shoes, a jacket, and maybe a blanket for a seated outdoor reflection.

A typical retreat done partly at home and partly outdoors might begin at home with an opening ritual, breakfast, and the first contemplative exercises; continue with a gratitude walk and nature hike, including lunch; and conclude with a closing ritual done in the quietude of one's own home or room.

However you choose to spend your day alone, it should be somewhere you can be apart physically, emotionally, and electronically from daily distraction. This means no cell phone (except for emergencies), no e-mail, no texting, and, of course, no radio or television. Aging itself is a quiet affair; it doesn't broadcast its lessons at high volume. We feel its impact fully when the world around us is quiet enough that we can hear the sound of our own breathing. At those times we can perceive the inner clock that always keeps honest time—our own breath. That will be one of the contemplative reflections on your day away.

Equipment

For your day away you may want to use the following things:

Candle and Matches. I like to use a votive candle because it fits into a glass holder and is safe inside or outside. The candle represents illumination, spirit, aspiration, hope, the divine, and the eternal; as a spiritual symbol it is universal. The candle flame represents your divine spark.

Vase and Fresh Flowers or Other Greenery. Don't try to arrange them much. Let them arrange themselves. This is the Zen style of flower arranging. Flowers represent impermanence, beauty, and fragility—qualities of every living thing, including yourself. In that sense the flowers on the altar represent and reflect your own beauty.

Two Bowls. Select two bowls, one large and one small. These bowls, and the small objects they will contain, will represent the years of your life—past, present, and future—and the "before and after" of time, an important theme for the entire day.

Round Objects, Edible or Inedible. You will need eighty or so small round objects to represent the years of your life, past and future. These might be small stones, coins, buttons, or candies.

Bell. Sometimes I joke that you can't be a Buddhist without a bell. It is true that bells are everywhere in Buddhist centers, but bells as spiritual instruments are hardly unique to Buddhism; church bells are still a familiar Sunday morning sound in many communities. In a meditative context, the bell means "right now," "pay attention," "time to start," or "time's up." In a metaphorical sense, the bell marks time and alerts you.

Pen, Paper, Envelope, Journal, and Clock. Throughout the day you will be doing some writing. If you already keep a journal, use it. If not, find one you can dedicate to days away. (It probably goes without saying that a laptop, tablet computer, and smartphone are not suitable tools for this kind of writing.) In addition, you will need two pieces of notepaper in connection with the rituals that begin and end the day. The paper should not be scraps, but high quality. They will become ritual offerings, as much as the candle and flowers are. Before your day begins, you'll fold the notepaper and put it in the envelope. A clock and perhaps a timer are most useful in timing the various aspects and exercises of the day.

An Eight-Hour Day of Spirit

It is probably not ideal to begin your day away early with 6 A.M. e-mails, Web surfing, or phone calls and end it with a busy evening of social engagements. However you plan the day, try to ensure that it will be one of reflection and quiet. For those who cannot find eight continuous hours for quiet reflection, do a half day. One of my mundane spiritual slogans is that something is always better than nothing.

Now that you have gathered what you need, you are ready to begin.

CHAPTER 13

A Day Away— The Morning

Breakfast

Begin your day away with breakfast at a time you've designated—say, 9 A.M.—understanding that eating itself can be a spiritual practice. From saying grace before meals to a full-fledged monastic eating ritual, the taking of food is one of the principal ways we express and embody our connection with all living things. In the Zen monastery where I was trained, each meal was a ritual of mindful awareness. Unfolding a set of cloth-wrapped eating bowls, we ate the food slowly, in silence and in meditation posture, fully attending to the taste of each bite. Shunryu Suzuki made many adjustments to our monastic life to make it more suitable for Americans, but when it came to the eating ritual he insisted on the traditional way. He taught us how the true taste of the food comes through when we are not talking, not reading, not concentrating on anything other than the food itself. I never appreciated the gift of food more than during those training years.

So if you are at home and can be alone in the kitchen, prepare your meal mindfully, handling the food carefully and moving around the kitchen slowly. When you sit down to eat, just eat: Don't do anything else. Even the simplest food is a gift from so many plants and animals; even water and air are miracles we rarely think of.

If you are at a hotel, order breakfast from room service, and when it comes lay it out on a table so that each item has its own space. If you are having breakfast outside, lay out the food with the same care. When all is ready, say a simple grace. The Buddhist grace in my tradition is, "We venerate the three treasures [the teacher, the teaching, and the community] and give thanks for this food, the work of many people and the sacrifice of every form of life." If you prefer, it can be a prayer from your own religious tradition.

Stop and reflect: How many thousands of meals have you eaten in the course of your whole life? How often have you stopped in this way to be alone with your food in full appreciation of it? The world has worked hard to nourish you these many decades. One-fifth of the world's population begins and ends the day hungry. When we eat mindfully we are connected to these multitudes of hungry people.

After breakfast, clean your dishes and eating area. You may want to prepare lunch now for later in the day. A

sandwich, fruit, and a bottle of water or fruit drink may suffice. Add some crackers, peanut butter, or cheese for snacks.

I typically suggest forty minutes for breakfast preparation, eating, lunch prep, and cleanup. Once cleanup is
complete, it should be about 9:40.

A Simple Ritual

When I ask people in my workshops about ritual, some say
they don't like ritual, and that the religious rituals of their
childhood seemed inauthentic or not meaningful to them.

I always encourage people to set aside such memories. A
ritual is a direct expression of the inner life, an activity that
expresses more deeply what ordinary words cannot. We all
have a natural ability to create ritual; children do it all the
time. Their jump-rope songs and movements—whether
learned from a previous generation or created on the
spot—are one familiar example. In that spirit, the ritual I
propose is not specifically Buddhist, but it is symbolic of
what you are about to do—retreat from the flow of your
ordinary routines in order to step into a different river.

For your ritual you will erect an altar. You'll need a candle, a vase, flowers, the two bowls, your pen and two pieces
of notepaper, and the eighty or so small round objects.

The altar should be set up in a place apart—in an alcove
at home, on a table in a hotel room, on a flat rock in the
outdoors.

Set your flowers or branches or grasses in the vase with
water. Place the candle on the altar and light it. Now count

out your pebbles or candies—one for each year you have lived—and set them in the large bowl in front of the flowers and candle. Set the empty small bowl to the right of the large bowl.

This completes the setup for the ritual, but before I describe the ritual itself I want to tell you a story from the Zen tradition that speaks about the years of a human life.

Sun-Face Buddha, Moon-Face Buddha

Zen Master Baso was ill. There were rumors that he was dying, but no one knew for sure. An old friend of Baso's, the abbot of a nearby temple, came to visit him. He entered Baso's sickroom and said, "How are you?"

Baso replied, "Sun-face Buddha, moon-face Buddha."

According to Buddhist scripture, the sun-face Buddha lived for a thousand years, while the moon-face Buddha lived for only one day and night. Baso was saying he did not know how long he was going to live—for another day, or for many more years.

This was one of Shunryu Suzuki's favorite Zen teaching stories. Suzuki had told us how frail he himself was as a boy, and about the hardships he underwent during World War II. He had not expected to live to sixty, so that now, at the age of sixty-five, with so many young followers in America, he was happy. Commenting on Baso's statement, Suzuki said, "Master Baso was enjoying his life, breath by breath and moment by moment. Whatever happened, he was ready."

———

The flowers on your altar are like moon-face Buddhas. Their fragility makes them beautiful. The large bowl full of pebbles or candies, each representing a year of your life, is like sun-face Buddha—so many years you have lived already! Now take up the empty smaller bowl and reflect on the life left to you. Ask yourself, "How many more years do I have to live?"

What are you hoping for? What would you be content with? Suppose you had only a year, or a month, or a week or a day. How would you feel?

Three months before Suzuki's death, he said, "Because of you, I ask Buddha for ten more years. If I have ten more years, all of you will be strong teachers and can carry on. I pray to Buddha for this." Three months later he was gone, his prayer unanswered. But just because Baso, or Suzuki, or you or I can accept however long or short our life is doesn't mean that we don't love our life, and the life of all those close to us, and want it to continue for as long as possible.

As human beings, it is so. So now, mindful of this, count out into the small bowl the number of pebbles that represent the years you hope or imagine are left to you. This is your offering to your own future as sun-face or moon-face Buddha. The pebbles of your future years are a wish, like wishing on a star. We know that wishes do not always come true, but counting out the pebbles gives the thought a star-like sparkle. This day is like every day—you can't know about tomorrow, but today you are here.

The beginning ritual continues: Take out your pen and the two pieces of paper. On the first piece of paper, write:

AGING BREATH BY BREATH

AGING LOVING KINDNESS

AS I GROW OLDER, MAY I BE KIND TO MYSELF;

AS I GROW OLDER, MAY I ACCEPT JOY AND SORROW;

AS I GROW OLDER, MAY I BE HAPPY AND AT PEACE.

AS EACH OF US GROWS OLDER…

AS ALL BEINGS GROW OLDER…

And then list the contemplative reflections you will be doing in the course of the day:

GRATITUDE WALK

GRATITUDE JOURNAL

DOING NOTHING IS DOING SOMETHING

VERTICAL TIME

RESTING IN AWARENESS

DISSOLVING THE CIRCLE

On the second piece of paper, write two things: first, what seems to you to be your biggest problem, then what you clearly see is your greatest joy.

My biggest problem is _____

My greatest joy is _____

Fold the two pieces of paper and replace them in the envelope. If you have written out your goals and expectations for the day as suggested in the last chapter, put that in the envelope too, and put the envelope in your pocket. They will be your companions for the day, and at day's end there will be a similar ritual to part with them.

Now, in a whisper, or silently to yourself, repeat the first line of the Loving Kindness aspiration prayer three times:

As I age, may I be kind to myself.

Blow out the candle. Gently touch a flower petal or leaf—each of them a moon-face Buddha. It should be around 10:00. The ritual of beginning is complete.

One Breath at a Time

Next, locate an area that will be your contemplative "home" for the day, where you can set out your meditation chair or cushion. If you are at home or at a hotel, your "spot" can be close to your altar. If you are outside, find a sheltered spot beneath a tree—the Buddha is often depicted sitting under a tree—or near a large rock.

Your first contemplation will be Aging Breath by Breath, which you might have reviewed during your preparations. The essence of that contemplation is first, that our experience of time is mutable; second, the breath is our inner clock, rhythmical and steady; and third, though we experience our aging in many ways, we actually age only one breath at a time.

Today you will perform this practice a bit differently than in Chapter 2. Setting up your altar and performing your beginning ritual has begun a process of withdrawal and disengagement. You have left behind your world of everyday routines and entered a different world. Aside from being the way we organize and manage time, routines can also be our way of not having to deal with time's shadow: our mortality. While breaking routine may be refreshing, it also can bring some tension or discomfort. It might be too strong to say that we are "addicted" to our everyday routines, but we are certainly habituated to them.

This is true for me too. Every day, as soon as I get up, I brew a pot of shade-grown green tea. I use a Japanese tea service that includes a cherrywood tea canister, a handmade Japanese ceramic pot, a bowl for cooling the hot water, and a cup. I am acclimated to the good feeling that comes with this morning tea ritual and look forward to it every day. I don't think about it much until I travel. Then when I wake up in an unfamiliar hotel room I notice I am grumpy. Where is my green tea? Where is my favorite teapot? Your day away is like this, a major breach of routine. Don't be surprised if you're less than comfortable.

To begin this meditation, ring your bell three times and tune in to your breath as your inner clock. This meditation lasts twenty minutes, as you focus on one breath at a time. Think of each breath as a bite of food. It enters and offers its taste. You experience the taste, whatever it is. If you suddenly have an urge to run down to Starbucks and have a grande latte, appreciate the "taste" of that impulse. If you think, "This personal retreat is silly; I have better things to do," appreciate that taste too—one breath at a time, one taste at a time. "When you meditate," Suzuki used to say, "You are always the boss of your life." The boss is the one who sees clearly what is going on. The boss lives his or her life one breath at a time and isn't surprised or shocked that some of the employees want to run to Starbucks. The boss can relax. "Not doing your ordinary routines today, I see," he or she can say with a chuckle. "Well, you can call this a day away if you want, but to be honest, it's really all the other days that are days away. Here is where your true home is, right here. Welcome home!"

Twenty minutes of meditation should refamiliarize yourself with the breath as your real home. When you are done, ring your bell, bow if you like, and slowly get up. It should be about 10:30.

Take a break. Wherever you are, walk around, look at what is around you. As one of my meditation teachers used to say when we were on a break, "Don't meditate!" What he meant was, don't have in your mind that you are doing anything special. As much as possible, don't have anything in your mind. Dogs and children, when they are exploring a new place, don't have too many thoughts about it. They are too busy exploring!

Take about fifteen minutes to explore the way a child explores. Then sit down comfortably in a chair. It is now 10:45.

Ring your bell three times.

Aging Metta

As I grow older, may I be kind to myself;
As I grow older, may I accept joy and sorrow;
As I grow older, may I be happy and at peace.

This is the prayer of Loving Kindness—the Buddhist term is "metta"—that we discussed in Chapter 7. During your personal retreat, you will be using this prayer several times during the day.

Take out the piece of paper on which you wrote this prayer earlier in the day and hold it in your lap.

Read it off the paper a few times to yourself.

Close your eyes and see if you now know it by heart.

Open your eyes and read it off the paper again.

For the next fifteen minutes you will be reciting this prayer. You can do it silently or in a low voice. You can do it with eyes closed from memory, or eyes open, reading from the page.

Each of these ways has its own flavor, and during the fifteen minutes, I encourage you to try all of them. When you read it off the page in your own handwriting, there is a sense of receiving the prayer from outside. When you close your eyes and recite by heart, the prayer may seem to come more from the body, engaging the throat and the heart.

When you are finished, ring your bell and reflect on what you've done and how you feel.

Even though "you" have stopped reciting, the words of

Loving Kindness will continue reverberating. Allow time for that to happen, and in particular to appreciate the emotional qualities of the words "aging," "kind," "joy," "sorrow," "happy," "peace."

AGING

KIND

JOY

SORROW

HAPPY

PEACE

Write them down in your journal if you like. The prayer has syntax like any sentence, but these key words are like dreams: They sink deep.

We'll be returning to this prayer again as the day progresses. For now just let it settle and come to rest.

It should be around 11:00. Time for tea.

Tea

If you are a tea drinker like me, now is the time to fix yourself some tea. Or choose some other beverage. Tea or coffee, caffeinated or not, hot or cold, juice, water, soda—it is your choice. As with breakfast, prepare it mindfully and in silence. Clean up carefully. Take your drink and return to your "spot."

Doing Nothing Is Doing Something

As you finish your cup of tea, clean up, stand up, and look around. Wherever you are, whatever the surroundings, I ask that for the next fifteen minutes you do . . . nothing at all.

This is not as easy as it sounds.

Remember the instruction of my old meditation teacher: "Don't meditate!" This exercise goes further—here you don't do anything. I can't tell you how to do this, because then that would be having you do something. You have to figure out what "doing nothing" means for you.

Is it all right for you to walk around? You decide; but whatever you do, don't do anything. Can you look at the paintings on the walls, or the furniture in the room, the brambles and briars beside you on a walking trail? You can if you want, but is that doing something? Can you spend some time looking at the objects on your altar: the flowers, the candle, the two bowls with their pebbles or candies in them?

Certainly you can, as long as you don't do anything.

You may find this exercise silly, pointless, or a waste of time. (That's an odd expression. What is "wasting" time, anyway?) You may be right. Even if you are, how does that change the exercise? You still have to fill up the fifteen minutes with—nothing. You're welcome to feel any way you like, as long as you don't make your feelings into doing something.

You might just approach the exercise the way a child

would. Young children don't have jobs, responsibilities, people to call, appointments to keep, or things to do. How do they figure out what to do next? How do *you* figure it out? It may help to remember those times when you were a child, by yourself, with "nothing" to do, and try to recall what that meant and how it felt.

Once your fifteen minutes are up, return to your spot. It is now about 11:30. Ring your bell three times. At last you can do something!

Gratitude Walk

The Gratitude Walk of Chapter 4 is an exercise in noting and noticing. Remember the Chinese monk who bowed to everything in gratitude as he walked? That is the spirit of this exercise: to see each thing you notice as an opportunity for gratitude. If you like to write down what you notice as you walk, the way bird-watchers do, take your journal with you. Otherwise, there will be time on your return to jot down your observations.

Your thoughts of gratitude can begin as soon as you stand up to go out. To stand, to walk, and to move are themselves something to be grateful for. This was the first lesson I learned when I woke up in the hospital after two weeks in a coma, unable even to sit up or turn over in bed. I was utterly forlorn and despairing, fearing that I would never walk again—until my doctor came in and expressed real delight that I could wiggle my fingers and toes.

"Fantastic!" she said. "You have no idea what a good thing that is."

She was right. I didn't. But eventually I did, and as you walk around your neighborhood, or in the park, or on the beach, or wherever you decide to take your gratitude walk, notice the very abilities to walk, to see and hear, and to reflect as the great miracles they are.

Walk for twenty to thirty minutes, noticing, noting, and perhaps writing. On your return, it should be about noon, and either in your head or on paper, you should have a list. It might look something like this:

WALKING—A BODY THAT STILL WORKS!

LUPEN, BLOOMING IN OCTOBER, STILL TRYING.

A SCRUB JAY, BEAK CLUTCHING A TWIG FOR A NEST.

SUNNY SKY—GOOD WEATHER!

HAVEN'T THOUGHT ABOUT MONEY ALL MORNING.

Gratitude Reflections

Come back to your spot, sit down, and ring your bell three times. If you have been writing as you walk, open your journal and review what you have written. If you have waited to jot down your observations of gratitude, do that now.

Then simply read over your list, not once or twice, but three times. Treat it like a spontaneous poem. Notice the way that reading it over, or reciting it in a low voice to yourself, has a different quality than its first writing. Read it again; it is a message to yourself from yourself, from your "boss" to you. The message says, "This is the way life really is when you take time to notice. The simplest things count for a lot. Every day, every hour is actually like this. Try to remember this always."

Notice also as you read how many of your gratitude reflections concern fragile, fleeting things—a flower past its prime, a cloud in the shape of a dragon dissipating as you watch it, a dead garter snake by the side of the path. Everything changes, nothing lasts, and life goes on. This is the truth that the next practice in your day away will illuminate.

Prayer for the Passing Away of Things

As we did earlier in the day, sitting in your spot, take out the paper on which you wrote the Metta prayer and for ten minutes recite silently to yourself or in a low voice the following version of the prayer:

> *As everything ages and passes away, may each of*
> *us be kind to ourselves;*
>
> *As everything ages and passes away, may each of*
> *us accept joy and sorrow;*
>
> *As everything ages and passes away, may each of*
> *us be happy and at peace.*

Notice how the prayer has changed and expanded. We are now not saying "As I grow older . . ." but "As everything ages and passes away . . ." It is not just that you are aging, with all the particularity of your feelings about that, but that everything is aging. What is happening to you is happening to everyone and everything around you. And your aspiration is not just "May *I* be kind to myself," but may *everyone* be that way.

Remember the Buddha's teaching of the mustard seed? He asked the mother whose baby had died to visit every house in the village, looking for one that had been spared such sorrow. The mother found that everyone shared her grief. The feeling of this prayer is something like that. Or, in the vernacular of today, we are all in this together.

After you have finished the Metta prayer, ring your bell three times.

It's lunchtime.

CHAPTER 14

A Day Away—
The Afternoon

Lunch

Find a quiet spot, whether inside or out, and spread out your food in a mindful fashion. With the gratitude walk still fresh in your mind, seeing the food before you should stimulate those same grateful feelings. As at breakfast, say the Buddhist grace: "We venerate the three treasures and give thanks for this food, the work of many people and the contributions of every form of life," or any mealtime grace that you are accustomed to.

Before you begin your meal, this is a good time to practice "listening" to your stomach. Are you actually hungry? You may be. Surprisingly, contemplative exercises are real work and stimulate the appetite. Try to remain conscious of the stomach's wisdom as you eat your meal. Remember the Japanese expression "80 percent full" and the French saying "I have no more hunger." If you are trying to eat less and have had difficulty tuning in to your stomach, you may find it easier today. A morning spent in mindful silence opens the channels of energy and receptivity throughout your body.

Doing Nothing—Again!

I have led meditation retreats for nearly thirty years, and as I think back to all those different retreats, the time just after lunch is most interesting to observe. People have typically gotten up quite early, and so by lunchtime they are tired. Having just eaten a meal makes them even more sleepy. The time after lunch is open and unscheduled, and so people scatter hither and yon to rest. If the weather is warm, you can see people lying on the grass or sitting under trees. Inside the meditation hall, people tuck the meditation cushions under their heads and try to nap. If it is a residential retreat, most people disappear to their rooms. It is all officially silent, so what I see is a grand tableau of a large group of people doing . . . nothing!

I have sometimes wondered what it would be like to lead a whole day retreat where from morning until night it is lunchtime break! Now that it is that time for you, I urge you to give in to being completely relaxed. There is nothing to do, nowhere to go, and the feeling is "betwixt and between." But betwixt and between what? Between what has come before and what will come after, of course. But that is true of every hour, every minute, and every moment. What is special about this particular hiatus that gives us permission to let go completely?

This is, I believe, a rather deep question, but you need not ponder it now. Just rest—as completely as you can. We will take up the quality of "resting completely" in the contemplative reflection that concludes the day.

Wake yourself up at around 12:45, go back to your spot, ring your bell three times, go to your altar, and light the candle. It is time to practice vertical time.

Vertical Time

I first described the vertical time contemplation at the conclusion of Chapter 5, so you may want to refer back to that section now. This is in part a breath meditation, so return to your spot, again ring the bell three times, and adopt a meditation posture comfortable for you.

Today's practice of vertical time will be a little different from the method I described earlier. You have spent the past few hours in contemplative silence: looking, watching, sensing, feeling. What has that done to your sense of time? As you sit quietly in meditation posture, reflect on the feeling of the past several hours. Does it feel like several hours? Does it feel longer; is there a sense that time has expanded and stretched itself out? Does it feel shorter—does "time fly," as the expression goes?

I have often written here that time is the essence of aging, but what does that really mean? As I originally described the practice of vertical time, I asked you to imagine the past stretching off to the left. But this morning we created another way to visualize the past: the pebbles, seeds, or candies in the large bowl, each one representing a year of life. As you sit quietly now, bring to mind the moment you counted out those markers of your years, and in your mind's eye do it again. The first marker is year one, a year you almost certainly do not remember, but in a way is the most important, since it is the day and date you first came into this world and this body. The second and third markers are much the same. Only the faintest and fleetest memories remain of that time, but one thing you know for certain—some adult, in most cases a parent, was watching over you and taking care of you.

In your mind's eye, let each marker of years drop from your hand into the bowl, picturing some highlight or remembrance from that year as you do. One by one let them all pass from hand to bowl until they are all there—your whole life, represented now by this body, sitting in this spot at this exact time.

This is the life you have lived; this is the age you are. There is an absoluteness and trustworthiness to this fact. Shunryu Suzuki's affirmation bears repeating: "Which is more real, your problems or the fact that you are here right now? That you are here right now is an ultimate fact."

Take a few breaths, each time exhaling completely into the bottom of your cushion or the bottom of the chair. It is true; that you are here right now is an ultimate fact, and each exhale confirms it. The exercise of mentally counting out each year of your life is a way of mapping the horizontal dimension of time, but all of that dissolves into the "up and down" of each exhale. With each breath the particularity of your history—"the things that happened to happen"—dissolves into the ultimate fact of your being here in this moment.

In a few moments you will shift your attention to the second bowl on your altar—your imagined future. But before you do, let your recollection of the past continue to settle. Ordinarily we carry the past and its memories like a sack full of stones. Our tendency is to drag that sack with us through the doorway of each new day. Right now, breath by breath, is a chance to let all of that go. (You don't always have to carry that sack of stones, by the way; in each moment it is your choice.)

When you are ready, turn your attention to the second bowl and the feelings you had when you counted the year markers into it. Go back and in your mind's eye do it again. The first marker is next year. What thoughts come to mind as that one goes in? The next marker is the year after next. What does that bring to mind? Does the whole exercise make you uneasy? Is it possible that you feel a little resentment at being asked to do it at all?

How many markers did you put in at the beginning of the day? Now that several hours have passed, do you still agree with yourself, or would you like to change the count? Would you put in fewer markers now, or more?

Let these reflections pass through you as you count out your future years, one by one, into the second bowl. This is a way of mapping horizontal time in the future.

When you are done, let all these thoughts dissolve, and

exhale into the bottom of your cushion or bottom of your chair. Whatever the number of markers you have put in, the future is unknown. Your anticipated future years will be marked with joys and sorrows. As Suzuki urges us, remember the ultimate reality of yourself right now.

Spend twenty to thirty minutes alternating between past time, future time, and present breath. With all the popular literature on the power of now and staying in the present moment, it is tempting to make a value judgment: "horizontal time bad, present moment good." Actually this is not so. There is no good or bad in our experiences of past, present, and future time. It is all your life, it is all your aging, and it is all true. Do not dwell in the past or worry about the future. The skill and the wisdom of this contemplative exercise is to develop the flexibility to move freely from one to the other without getting stuck.

When you have concluded your meditation, ring your bell three times and slowly get up. How do you feel? Do you feel any different: older, younger, or about the same? How do the number of markers in the second bowl, representing the years of your imagined future life, look to you now?

It's about 1:30 in the afternoon. Blow out the candle. Time for a walk.

Take a Walk

Shunryu Suzuki liked to say, "Don't be so serious!"

What he meant was, life is serious enough; no need to add to it. Turning the attention inward requires a lot of energy.

The secret of any successful meditation retreat—whether for a day, a week, or a month—is the alternation of intensity and release. Vertical time is an intense practice. So to release it, take yourself for a walk.

This is not a gratitude walk or a "doing nothing" walk. It is just a walk. The point of it is to move and to let go of any tension or intensity. It also contains a teaching that everywhere you go, mindful awareness goes with you. Even though you are not trying to concentrate, your day of meditative activity and reflection has left you in a concentrated state. Walking, as long as it is in silence, will not dissipate that concentration, but disperse it throughout your body and your senses.

So notice if your senses seem sharper now, if colors seem a bit more intense, if sounds seem more potent, if your movements feel more fluid. Experienced meditators often do sitting meditation for days, or even weeks, without moving around much. In the Zen tradition, we alternate periods of sitting with periods of walking—and sometimes that walking is fast and energetic. We also sometimes do movement meditation, such as Tai Chi. If you are schooled in any of the many meditative movement traditions, you can do that during this time in place of or in addition to walking.

Meditation is not just a respite from the commonplace; it is part and parcel of the commonplace. An ordinary walk in the park is not just ordinary. In one of the most famous Zen teaching stories, Joshu asked his teacher Nansen, "What is the path to awakening?" Nansen answered, "Ordinary activity is the path to awakening."

As with many Zen stories, this dialogue is so plain that it is hard to see the lesson in it. Joshu thinks that the path to awakening is something special or secret, a matter apart from the ordinary. Nansen reminds us that the path to awakening is whatever path we are on right now. As you take your walk, you walk the path of enlightenment. And actually, there is never any other path.

Thank You

On your return, visit your altar. Examine the flowers and the two bowls. Light the candle. Sit in a relaxed position at your spot and take out your journal. Read over all that you have written so far: your gratitude walk observations and any other notes you have taken during the day.

In an earlier chapter, I described the thanksgiving prayer, in which you said "thank you" to yourself and then watched to see what thought or image came to mind. Now we are going to do the thanksgiving prayer in reverse. Next to or after every gratitude note in your journal, write the words "thank you." Go down your list until every note has the words "thank you" next to it.

Now read it over to yourself and notice the way in which the addition of those two words makes what you have written a kind of incantation or prayer.

Once you have finished, from your envelope take out the paper on which you wrote the Metta prayer, and read in silence or in a low voice the third version of the prayer:

As all beings grow older, may they be kind to themselves;
As all beings grow older, may they accept joy and sorrow:
As all beings grow older, may they be happy and at peace.

Do this for about ten minutes, rest in silence for a few moments, and put the paper back in its envelope.

Take up your journal and open to the place of your last written reflection. What comes to mind now? How does it feel to take the Metta prayer that you began by directing toward yourself, and "pay it forward" to everyone else?

You may have some further reflections to note in your journal. As you do, remember to add the words "thank you" at the end of each.

When you are finished, close everything up, ring your bell three times, blow out the candle. It should be about three o'clock: tea time.

Tea

Prepare your beverage of choice as you did in the morning, and drink it quietly, concentrating on the taste. Remember the story of De Shan, the Diamond Sutra expert, and the tea lady. The tea lady had said to him, "Past mind, present mind, future mind are all in motion. With which mind will you drink this cup of tea?"

Your practice of vertical time earlier in the afternoon should help you do better than De Shan, and simply drink your tea with confidence and pleasure. The point is to not think about anything in particular and just drink your tea the same way you breathe—one sip at a time.

From one point of view, during the time it takes for you to finish your cup of tea or coffee, you've aged fifteen minutes—precious time that will never return! From another point of view, you have just enjoyed your tea in the continuing present, Blake's "eternity in an hour." In that sense, you haven't aged at all; you are just here.

Resting in Awareness

For the next hour, we will practice the most fundamental meditation of all—Resting in Awareness, as described in Chapter 10. It is a practice of utter relaxation and acceptance, which is why it is both the simplest and most profound of all meditations. You will accomplish the practice in three stages: concentration, spaciousness, and surrender. Each stage is fifteen minutes long, and punctuated by a short break. You may want to use a timer to help you know when each fifteen-minute period is up, or try to sense the passage of time inwardly.

As always, light the candle, ring your bell three times, and sit at your spot in a comfortable meditation posture with half-open eyes. As you now know, most meditation has two aspects: focus and insight. Resting in Awareness includes both aspects. The first stage of the practice will emphasize focus. Traditionally we concentrate on the breath as our preparation for Resting in Awareness.

As we have done with many of the contemplative reflections, begin by tuning in to the breath as though to a radio station. The breath consists of inhaling, exhaling, and a pause or resting space before the next inhalation comes. Spend some time focusing your attention on this threefold rhythm: inhale, exhale, pause; inhale, exhale, pause.

The three stages of breath need not be equal in time. When you are at rest, it is common for inhaling to be rather quick, exhaling to be more prolonged, and the pause after exhaling to also be quick or short. For the purpose of this contemplation, the pause following exhaling is the most important. That pause is a kind of expanse or open space, like a field or a meadow. Be sure that as you focus on the feeling of it, you do not elongate it or force it to wait. That would introduce tension into what should be a calming and relaxing process.

It may be helpful to think of the post-exhalation pause as a kind of melting or "spreading" of the breath out beyond your body and into the space of the room or area where you are sitting. With each breath, relax into exhaling and the pause that follows with a sense of melting or surrender. As Lama Surya Das likes to say, "Let go and let be." Let go of each breath as it leaves you, let the space that follows be just as it is, and let each inhale come back just when it wants to.

If you find yourself becoming distracted, imagine those distractions dissolving into the open space that follows each exhale. Let them go and let them be.

When the timer rings, slowly open your eyes fully, take a couple of deep breaths, and slowly begin to move and stretch. When you feel ready, slowly stand up, remaining in your spot. Let the concentrated feeling of your breath continue to flow through your body as you stand. To stand quietly in this way is itself an act of meditation. Many traditions of meditative movement, such as Tai Chi, include the practice of standing in calmness like this.

After a few minutes, sit down again in meditation posture. You are ready to move on to the next stage of the practice, which is "spaciousness."

As we discussed in Chapter 10, conscious awareness resembles space, in that it has no specific shape or boundary. It doesn't have any content of its own, either. Rather, it contains and accepts whatever content comes into it, whether a thought, a feeling, or an emotion. Conscious awareness differs from physical space, however, in that it is awake and alive: It is conscious.

The breath can be experienced as a kind of moving space. The breath, like space and like awareness, has no form or shape either, but you can feel it flow in and out, and after exhaling it dissipates into the wider space all around you.

So now, as you resume your meditation, notice the assumption behind the breath that *you* are the one breathing, and turn it on its head, saying to yourself instead, "This breath is breathing me." Picture the space around you as expanding and contracting you the way an accordion player expands and contracts the accordion's bellows. Imagine yourself as the passive recipient, from the wider world all around you, of this wonderful thing called breath.

As you develop this image and adjust to it, let your awareness shift to be less on the movement of breath in and out, and more on the space in which breath moves. See how large and expansive you can allow this space to be.

The space is breathing me. For the rest of this fifteen minute period, let this be your contemplative focus. Relax into the space that is breathing you, and as you let the space do its work, surrender to its efficiency and power. There is nothing you need to do. Space itself is doing the work of expanding awareness beyond the envelope of the physical body.

As the fifteen minutes ends, once again open your eyes fully, slowly stretch, come to standing, and stand quietly for another five minutes.

The third stage of this meditation is Resting in Awareness. As you sit down and resume your meditation posture, let all thoughts of breath and all images of space disappear, and just rest in the state of being that you have become. Let everything go. Don't try to meditate; don't try to focus. Don't try to do anything. At this moment, there is nothing to do, nothing to accomplish, nothing to achieve. You are complete just as you are. If thoughts come, they too are complete just as they are. If feelings of impatience or distraction come, let them come. They too are complete.

This is complete surrender. You might ask, surrender to *what*? We could say, surrender to a higher or deeper power, but that idea isn't necessary. Whatever is higher or deeper is already complete within you. You are it and it is you. Relax, trust, and have faith that the power of this deepest of relaxation is always with you, can always be called upon, and, if summoned, will always answer your call.

This is your highest self, but it is also your most ordinary self.

When your fifteen minutes are up, open your eyes wide and gently come back into movement and then to standing.

You are complete, and the hour is concluded.

Dissolving the Circle

You may be familiar with the elaborate sand paintings Tibetan Buddhist monks do as part of their religious ritual. The Navajo and other Native Americans have this practice too. They spend hours or days carefully constructing an elaborate image from colored sand. But once their ritual is complete, they destroy the image, collect all the sand into a heap, and ceremonially disperse it.

In that same spirit, as your day away comes to a close, you will appreciate one last time what you have made and done, and then disperse it into the place from whence it came.

Open your envelope and take out your aspiration for the day, the one that went:

When I return from my day away I will be _____
_____ and I will do the
following:_____
_____.

How did you do? Was your hope for the day fulfilled? If not, or if there is more you feel needs to be done, that then becomes the day's lesson and new aspiration. As for your promise for the future, is that a promise you can keep?

Reflect on your state of mind when you wrote it and your state of mind now. Nothing ever goes exactly according to plan, but plans have a way of working out nonetheless.

Now examine the piece of paper on which you wrote:

My biggest problem is _____
My greatest joy is _____

Are these statements still true? Has anything changed? Sometimes a seemingly intractable problem grows more workable after a day of quiet reflection. And the inventory of familiar pleasures can grow or change in the time and space of a day away. See what is true for you now, especially around the shape and dimension of your aging.

Your envelope with its aspirations and intentions is the sand painting of your day away. The time has come to dissolve it. If you have the wherewithal to burn it, do that, letting it disappear into flame and smoke. If you would like to tear your writings into little pieces, that is another way to make them vanish. However you physically dispense with the memorabilia of your day, allow your mind to also let them go. They have served their purpose, and that purpose is now done.

At your altar, pour the pebbles from the smaller bowl into the larger one. Your past, present, and future life are again one. Blow out the candle; ring your bell three times.

Your day away is complete.

CHAPTER 15

Final Thoughts

As I was in the final stages in the writing of this book, I happened to run into Alan and Christina at a coffee shop. I had not seen them for several months. Accepting their invitation to join them, I noticed that Alan had put on a little weight and that Christina had cut her hair. Both of them seemed more serious.

They asked me how my book was coming along and I told them it was almost done and that they both were in it. "Oh dear," Christina said with mock dismay. "So much has changed since we talked to you back then."

Over the next twenty minutes, they told me that shortly after our conversations, they had decided to enter couples therapy. "We were headed in different directions," Alan said, "and hadn't really noticed. Once we got started in the therapy it was amazing what came out." Alan had come to realize how much it bothered him that his career had plateaued, just as Christina's seemed to be taking off. Christina saw the same problem from the other side. Alan's down mood was a drain on her, and she felt guilty for resenting him.

Meanwhile Christina heard from the gallery in New York that they had decided not to take her work. Shortly after that her she had another local show and this time sales were disappointing. "Suddenly we were both in the soup," Christina said. "Neither of us was getting what we wanted."

Alan said, "You remember that stress-reduction class I got into to help with my blood pressure? Well, I decided to take the training to be a stress-reduction instructor myself. I want to specialize in aging jocks like myself. All my sports friends are stressed out. They think they're thirty and they're on the wrong side of fifty. I can help these guys. I know what makes them tick."

I remembered what my psychiatrist friend had said: "When people get to the 'other side of the hill' in the second half of life, the world doesn't hand them a new identity anymore. They have to create it for themselves." That was what Alan was in the process of doing.

And he did follow through on his plan. Before long I began seeing his ad in the local paper: Stress Reduction for Aging Athletes. Alan had found something new for himself, and at the same time a way to give back.

A few weeks after seeing Alan and Christina, I got a call from Jacob, the oldest son of Sarah, the very elderly weaver

I introduced in Chapter 2. Sarah had passed away unexpectedly—if that can be said of someone 105 years old—and peacefully, in her sleep. She had left her affairs in meticulous order. In the top drawer of her desk was a folder marked "In the event of my death." In it, in addition to insurance policies, safe deposit box keys, and other essentials, was an envelope marked "Funeral." And in that envelope was a note to me, which Jacob read to me over the phone:

Dear Lew,

Well, by the time you read this I will be no more. I have been gifted with far too many years; I wonder sometimes if that has been a burden to my family. In any event, that's not my problem now. I have outlived three husbands, innumerable doctors, and even more numberless cats. What a chuckle! And now it's time for the last thing—to say my final good-bye. I've never been much for churches, they're mostly too solemn for my taste. I like the Buddhists, they seem to be a little more down-to-earth about things. Anyway I would like you to do me a favor and conduct my memorial service. We don't know each other that well, but I've come to meditation a few times and you've heard all about my life and my art, and I think you could do this for me without making more trouble for everyone than I already have.

So I hope you'll agree. Jacob can be your partner; he's always been a good boy (Ha! He's almost eighty.) and responsible. Don't do anything fancy, just let people know I had a good life and left it with no regrets. And take care of my family—all of them down to little Sarah my youngest great-great-granddaughter, who is fourteen months as I write.

Thanks for doing this. You asked me once what it was like to be 105, and for a moment I got testy with you. Well, my apologies. You're a good egg, and the only clergy person (or whatever they call them now) that I know. This is what it's really like to be 105; you have to write a letter like this and stick it in an envelope.

> Good luck,
> *Sarah*

P.S. Warning: I have a very large family.

I met with Jacob, and when he brought out an elaborate family tree on a paper as big as a city map, I realized that Sarah wasn't exaggerating. The immediate family, five generations not including cousins, numbered more than a hundred people.

Usually when I prepare for a memorial service I meet with the family to get a sense of their relationships, their emotional needs, and the kind of ceremony they would prefer. With Sarah's family this was not difficult. There was not much grief among them. Everyone I talked to seemed inclined toward a celebration of Sarah's long life. Though they were sad to see her go—particularly her grandchildren, who loved to hear stories about a time when there were still horses on the streets and telephones were hand-cranked—they were determined to send her on her way with the same quirky good humor that Sarah brought to everything she did.

In the end, the memorial service mostly organized itself, with each family member playing a part. There were songs, a slide show, and cookies and cakes baked from Sarah's own recipes. Her weavings hung at various heights across the front of the church, each with a destination: a few to shops and galleries where she had exhibited, the rest to specific descendants, including the very youngest. I recited a few Buddhist prayers. I ended with the one on Loving Kindness, which I know Sarah especially liked. Her three children each gave homilies, and each of her great-grandchildren brought offerings from nature—a pine branch, a buckeye, a caterpillar in a jar to represent Sarah's love of the outdoors.

When it was my turn to say something about Sarah, I described our meeting, my nervousness, my silly question, "What's it like to be 105?" and how after she forgave me for that, the tour of her house that she took me on.

Her weavings hung everywhere in the house. I recognize many of them here today. We stopped at every one. As she described each of them and told me about the yarn she used and where it had been spun, she reached out and touched the pieces. She stroked them and twirled their fringes in her fingers. Each of those weavings was part of her, and though she had finished them and named them, they were still alive and fresh for her.

In the course of writing my book, I have studied people like Sarah—the so-called extraordinary elderly. What makes these people extraordinary is not necessarily their advanced age, but their indomitable attitude toward life. Like Sarah, they are often very creative, and they are almost always curious, always reaching out to sense and feel the world freshly. It is wonderful for all of us to celebrate the fact that Sarah lived longer than most of us can imagine—although her long life was filled with equal measures of tragedy and joy. But as I watched Sarah reach out to touch the yarn out of which she made her art—she even stood up on her tiptoes to smell the pieces—I thought: I'll bet Sarah has always lived her life like this. For her, everything was new—the yarn, her art, the many loves, disappointments, and adventures of her life—all new.

As we say our final good-byes to our good friend Sarah—mother, grandmother, great-grandmother, and great-great-grandmother—let us accept from her these final lessons—which were the principles she lived by. Cultivate an attitude of inquiry about everything, be alert and aware to learn something from every experience, and keep your eyes and ears open for simple pleasures.

And so, as this book concludes, I hope that, like Sarah's approach to her art, it will not be finished, but will continue to influence your elderhood, day by day and breath by breath. Hold on to the underlying principle of all we have learned here: to remain aware and awake, regardless of what is going on. Many of our strengths and faculties decline as we age, but our ability to pay attention can be practiced through the contemplations in these pages, and can persevere and even grow.

As the Buddha said so long ago, "Don't believe it because you have read it or because I say it. Believe only because you have tried it and found out for yourself that it is true."

ACKNOWLEDGMENTS

My deepest thanks go to Bill Shinker, publisher of Gotham Books, who launched my writing career fourteen years ago by publishing *Work as a Spiritual Practice,* and now—after so much water under the bridge—has chosen to publish me again. Also I offer heartfelt thanks to Lauren Marino, Gotham's editor in chief, who has been tirelessly enthusiastic and upbeat every step of the way, besides being one of my best fans!

Barbara Lowenstein, my literary agent, liked the book idea from the moment I pitched it to her, and in the intervening three years has overseen every aspect and detail of the project, from my first book proposal efforts to all sorts of editing and promotional details. Barbara is the kind of agent every author wants to have. She's not afraid to be candid, but she is always supportive and when she says "Terrific" you know she means it.

Doris Ober, editorial consultant *extraordinaire*, held my literary hand throughout the whole process—first as a "proposal doctor," helping to shape and clarify what was sometimes a gaggle of semi-lucid ideas, and never being shy about saying, "I don't understand what you are saying." She also pored over every word of every chapter, tightening here, loosening there, like a master watchmaker of the written word. Thanks to Doris for being an indispensable partner!

When I asked Sylvia Boorstein—Buddhist teacher, best-selling author, and lifetime fellow traveler—to write the foreword for this book, she did not hesitate. "I'll do it!" she exclaimed, and then added, "I'd enjoy doing it." Her own thoughts about aging begin this book, eloquently and intimately, as is her magic. Thanks, Sylvia!

Dr. Roger Walsh—psychiatry professor, Buddhist teacher, and author of more books and articles than I can count—offered a tremendous service to me and my readers by contemporaneously publishing an article summarizing all the latest research on healthy aging. Without Roger's diligence and thoroughness (and citations!) this book would be much the poorer.

Many people contributed their expertise and professional experience to the making of this book. I particularly want to thank Dr. Robert Belknap and Dr. Peter Walsh, both of whom gave generously of their time to share with me their lifetime of clinical expertise. Others who offered professional perspectives include Dr. Seymour Boorstein, Lama Palden Drolma M.F.T., Ruth Herron, Rev. Tony Patchell,

Candyce Powell M.P.T., Rev. Alan Senauke, Dr. Grace Schireson, and Dr. Peter Schireson. Thanks to all!

I also owe a great debt of gratitude to all the many interviewees, students, workshop attendees, and blogging and e-mail correspondents who each added their unique contribution to a topic that is both universal and personal; my thanks to each of them.

And finally, I would like to thank my wife, Amy. One morning at breakfast I said, "I think I might like to write another book. I wonder what it should be about?"

She replied, "What about aging?"

Of such small beginnings are ambitious projects born.

May all beings everywhere be happy.

NOTES

1 Michael Cant and Rufus Johnstone, *Proceedings of the Royal Society B* (December 22, 2010), cited in Wynne Parry, Why Women and Whales Share a Rich Post-Breeding Life, *Live Science*, November 30, 2010, http://www.livescience .com/9024-women-whales-share-rich-post-breeding-life .html. For further information see Grandmother hypothesis, Wikipedia, http://en.wikipedia.org/wiki/Grandmother_ hypothesis.

2 William H. Thomas, *What Are Old People For* (VanderWyk & Burnham, 2004), 36.

3 Shunryu Suzuki, *Not Always So* (HarperCollins, 2002), 27–28

4 R. Walsh, Lifestyle and mental health, *American Psychologist* (January 17, 2011). Advance online publication. doi: 10.1037/ a0021769.

5 Roger Walsh and Shauna L. Shapiro, The meeting of meditative disciplines and western psychology: A mutually enriching dialogue, *American Psychologist* 61 (2006), 227–239.

6 *Harvard Health Letter,* July 2010.

7 H. G. Koenig, M. E. McCullough, and D. B. Larson, *Handbook of Religion and Health* (Oxford University Press, 2001).

8 Shunryu Suzuki, *Not Always So* (HarperCollins, 2002), 56.

9 The Dalai Lama, *Cultivating Compassion,* tr. Jeffrey Hopkins (Broadway Books, 2001), 150.

10 F. Borgonovi, Doing well by doing good: The relationship between formal volunteering and self-reported happiness, *Social Science and Medicine* 66 (2009), 2,312–2,334.

11 S. Post and J. Niemark, *Why Good Things Happen to Good People: The Exciting New Research That Proves the Link Between Doing Good and Living a Longer, Healthier, Happier Life* (Broadway Books, 2007).

12 *Science News,* July 17, 2010.

13 Shunryu Suzuki, *Zen Mind, Beginner's Mind* (John Weatherhill, Inc., 1970), 112.

14 Ibid., 112.

15 Dalai Lama, *Essence of the Heart Sutra* (Wisdom Publications, 2005), 12.

16 Ibid., 14.

17 S. Brown, R. Nesse, A. Vinokur, and D. Smith, Providing social support may be more beneficial than receiving it, *Psychological Science* 14 (2003), 320–327.

18 Shunryu Suzuki, *Not Always So* (HarperCollins, 2002), 6.

19 Charles J. Holahan, Kathleen K. Schutte, Penny L. Brennan, Carole K. Holahan, Bernice S. Moos, and Rudolf H. Moos, Late-life alcohol consumption and 20-year mortality, *Alcoholism: Clinical and Experimental Research* 34, no. 11 (2010), 1961–1971, cited in John Cloud, Why do heavy drinkers outlive nondrinkers? *Time,* August 30, 2010, http://www.time.com/time/health/article/0,8599,2014332,00.html.

20 Nikos Kazantzakis, *Zorba the Greek* (Simon and Schuster, 1964), 310–311.